If I honor who I am,
I subsequently bring grace to what I am
and integrity sustainable in the face of mistakes tempered
by accountability, mutual consideration, and personal responsibility
that will help to maintain credibility and relevance.

To the contrary, if I fail to honor who I am,
I eventually will bring disgrace to what I am through mistakes that are unable
to be tempered by the mentioned properties of integrity due to the fatality
self-importance and self-indulgence will oftentimes cause to
undermine and cripple credibility and relevance.

When there is the moment of doubt and indecision, whether to bring forth
the inherent gifts of my character or serve a false sense of stability and
security that merely promises to achieve conditional credibility,
resist the impulse to pursue distortion and perversion just to
satisfy illusions associated with what I am externally:

It is wise to remember, the predictability of conflict will
make an appearance to usher forth an opportunity and its conclusion to
produce experiences culminating in either grace or dishonor.
To pursue stability, security, and continuity that to establish credibility solely based on what a
person is externally and possesses materially is to guarantee a life lacking in moral authority.

To pursue stability, security, and continuity that guarantees to establish
credibility primarily based on who an individual is inherently
is to assure a life efficient with moral authority.
In its place, an existence that heavily leans on the practice of greed, abuse,
and domination to sustain the gravity to what is being pursued:
conditional stability, security, and continuity.

The manifestation of either an empire or coalition will quickly take shape
when the relationship is based on one or the other, respect or credibility.

Lorenzo D. Leonard

I dedicate this literary body of work to the numerous life lessons, good, bad, and indifferent that have taught me and continue to teach me that genuine and sustainable credibility, relevance, and personal value are strictly derived from an inherent legitimacy. This type of legitimacy has absolutely nothing to do with any external and material factors, but everything to do with the education, development, and consistent practice of the innate merits of character.

CONTENTS

Foreword ix
Who Is the Stranger?

Introduction xiii
In The Beginning

Chapter One 1
The New Comfort Zone

Chapter Two 23
Credibility and Relevance

Chapter Three 53
Too Many Concessions!

Chapter Four 77
A Negative or Positive?

Chapter Five 107
Strength of Character or Impotency

Chapter Six 121
Respect or Credibility

Chapter Seven 141
Vulnerability and Transparency

Chapter Eight 165
The Issue of Impoverishment

Chapter Nine 193
Conclusion

Afterword 211
Works Cited 213

WHO IS THE STRANGER?

It is easier to walk by the homeless, unemployed, mentally challenged, or returning military veteran asking for a handout than to take the opportunity to provide a distinguishing moment that would improve the immediate despair. Because of *what* the individual represents externally and appears to be lacking materially, "the marginalized are overlooked, cast aside, and purposely censored by the passerby." The truth is, "strip away the materialism and the external differences, and the passerby and the marginalized become very similar." There is neither genuine credibility nor relevance in his or her eyes of the judged or in the eyes of those passing judgment.

It is interesting how the unfamiliar will have such a substantial influence on the process of separating the authentic from the pretentious. The role of the stranger will consistently be to initiate an engagement for the purpose of establishing credibility and relevance on a level that has nothing to do with *what* a person is externally and possesses materially.

Without knowing, the stranger can also provide an opportunity for the passerby to gauge whether there is depth to the words of love and appreciation as expressed to those within his or her inner circle.

The type of credibility pursued, conditional or unconditional, will be revealed by the words, used or not used, to either satisfy the expectations of an empire or confirm that a coalition of equals does, in fact, exist. It should be mentioned that the ability to reach such a determination requires an openness to introspective thought.

Who is the stranger? The stranger is the person who smugly attempts to portray him or herself with a relevance that exhibits nothing more than a capacity to promote self-importance and self-indulgence. This, while possessing a self-awareness of going down a path that clearly has a sign posted at its entrance: dead end.

Who is the stranger? The stranger is, of course, thyself. It is the authentic and genuine aspect of a person's being. It is soul; it is individuality; it is where real meaning and purpose are derived through the medium of his or her merits of character.

The stranger frequently is in close proximity to its likeness; the individual. The mission of the unfamiliar is to always remain prepared to help with merging the *who* factor or inherent credibility with the *what* factor of an individual. Irrespective of an individual's sole alliance to *what* he or she is, the stranger remains ready to be accepted as credible and relevant. To add on to the sole alliance, a partnership with *who* the individual is intrinsically involves boldness and an intensified effort.

However, until the unfamiliar within is embraced and accepted, the stranger from a different class, religion, ethnicity, race, gender, political ideology, economic standing, sexual orientation, or educational background cannot be recognized as credible or relevant: there simply is no context to operate from that is out of the realm of familiarity.

The role of the stranger is to help determine if relationships are merely established as utility and convenience or authenticity. The stranger offers opportunities to experience mutuality, transparency, and vulnerability. If the stranger is responded to as though he or she has credibility, which is more than mere respect, then there is clear evidence that the love and appreciation expressed to family, friends, and close associates are based on genuine and legitimate principles.

Conversely, credibility and relevance rooted in the basic declaration of self-importance and self-indulgence is minus a moral precept; everything goes in favor of self-interest. Destiny does not have to remain married to experiences, which are used to define him or herself by; good, bad or indifferent. When the qualities representing meritorious character become married to the individual, a definitive conclusion is reached. His or her destiny transitions from a proposition of chance to an intention with a certainty based on that which is good, rather than right. Credibility, relevance, and value are, thus redefined, which helps to make the transition more than just a possibility.

Lorenzo D. Leonard

IN THE BEGINNING

After man and woman awoke together on that miraculous morning to commence with humanity's existence, what took place later that day was the first act to injure the credibility of another person to preserve one's own reputation. Also ushered onto the human landscape were two major impediments to unity and collaboration that would, in subsequent centuries to come, seriously push humanity to the edge of complete insanity. Inequity and inequality are the two barriers that have severely impacted human relationship. Figuratively speaking, the legendary "Garden of Eden" is where dishonorable practices were originally initiated that would remain a vital part of humanity's relationship backdrop.

After being made aware by the originator of the "Garden" regarding the abundance of trees bearing reliable sustenance to eat, a warning was issued that required man's complete obedience. Situated in the midst of the "Garden" were two distinct trees: the "Tree of life" and the "Tree of Knowledge of good and evil." Man was encouraged to appreciate and to eat from all the trees in the "Garden," especially the "Tree of life." Fruit from the "Tree of life" would provide a basic awareness and admiration for the sacredness of human life. But, man was told not to touch nor eat any fruit from the "Tree of Knowledge of good and evil," which bears sustenance that would put in jeopardy his inherent credibility and life.

The following day, and without man having knowledge, a pass-erby, extremely skillful in seduction and persuasion, convinced woman to eat from the forbidden "Tree of Knowledge of good and evil." Woman knew of the reliable sustenance, and she was aware of the restrictions regarding which tree to eat from and which to stay clear. However, lacking an appreciation and understanding with respect to her inherent credibility made it easy for the woman to be seduced by the stranger. Inherent credibility for both man and woman were symbolized by their physical state of being naked in the "Garden" without any sense of shame and embarrassment. Due to a lack of understanding concerning inherent credibility, genuine character traits such as integrity, vulnerability and transparency could not be valued nor protected.

Consequently, to pass up an opportunity to be as a god in pos-session of knowledge pertaining to good and evil would not be an option. Later into the day, when man and woman were together, the same seductive and persuasive statements spoken to the woman by the stranger were articulated to the man by his counterpart. The fruit was noticeably appealing, and after being reassured of the har-vest tasting delicious, the third element of encouragement became the convincing statement. Man gladly received his bounty from the woman upon hearing how their eyes would be opened, as well as their understanding expanded regarding the knowledge of good and evil upon eating from its tree.

Still later that day, after eating from the "Tree of Knowledge of good and evil" and embracing a negative interpretation associ-ated with being naked, man and woman made aprons out fig leaves to cover themselves. Both were quick to accept that vulnerability, transparency, and humility are to be considered humiliating and discreditable.

Though the three character traits helped to round out an in-depth composite representing inherent credibility; the attributes were to be avoided. As the two hid amongst the trees, individually covered with fig leaves, the overseer returned to the "Garden." At first the overseer could not find the couple, and soon called out to the man asking his whereabouts. Man's response to the overseer was that they were hiding due to feeling shameful and embarrassed regarding being naked.

Man was asked by the overseer just how he came to know that he was naked. Man was also asked to be accountable as to whether he had eaten from the "Tree of Knowledge of good and evil," when he was expressly commanded not to commit this act. Man's historic response was thus: "The woman whom thou gavest to be with me, she gave me of tree, and I did eat." What can be assumed concerning the relationship between the man and woman was that he probably was fond of her. But, based on his quick response to the overseer, she had no credibility as a person in his eyes. Her credibility and relevance was too hastily casted aside in an attempt to save his own credibility.

Stepping back from the story to examine its various messages can help to understand the significance of character development, and its connection with attaining relationships based on a genuine sense of legitimacy. One message to take away from the story is how a person may like or have fond feelings towards another person, but considers that person's inherent credibility as irrelevant and lacking value. This is especially true when that person has yet to accept his or her inherent credibility and relevance. When the attributes of good character are considered as irrelevant to bring to a relationship, then aprons made out of fig leaves will do to conceal genuine identities.

The "Garden of Eden" fable provides a backdrop for the defining moment humankind decided to assign more credibility and relevance to *what* an individual is externally than to *who* an individual is intrinsically. The "Tree of life" could provide genuine credibility, and sustain human existence based on attributes that comprise the merits of good character; nothing to feel ashamed and embarrassed to live. Again, because neither man nor woman had developed an appreciation for their state of innocence or nakedness, it was easy to reject the authentic in favor of joining the god-like ranks. Fruit consisting of sincerity, simplicity, and meekness simply will not feed nor satisfy the appetite of the person interested in exercising his or her self-will for purposes of self-interest. The "Tree of knowledge of good and evil" will yield fruit with a single purpose, and that is to discredit and destroy.

Shortly after birth, innocence is sacrificed to the provisional gods of this world because there is no societal, cultural, or religious commitment to acknowledge the "Tree of life." The education to character development would bring this pledge to realization. Learning about his or her inherent credibility has everything to do with giving legitimacy to the "Tree of life." Instead, in its place with respect to education are examples after examples that reinforce the appropriateness of power, treachery, and abuse. Evil is the outgrowth of both self-will and self-interest. As a consequence, to being dominated by self-will and self-interest, hence, the creations of classism, racism, and sexism, and other means to attain external credibility and relevance. This is the chosen path for achieving credibility and relevance upon eating from the "Tree of knowledge of good and evil."

The "Garden" also reveals the first act to blame and place responsibility on someone or something, other than one's self, for personal decisions that have less than a good result. To put woman in a position of responsibility for man's loss of innocence and inability to stand alone in his decision-making process in response to the overseer's questions, has historic ramifications.

Without the education to meritorious character, accountability, transparency, and integrity will consistently disclose an unwillingness to take responsibility for decisions deficient in favorable conclusions that were born out of self-will and self-interest. As previously mentioned, man's willingness to destroy his partner's credibility in order to keep intact his own legitimacy reveals another significant histori-cal act that plagues humankind in this modern era. Self-preservation will prove treacherous when the attempt is made to prove one's own credibility by destroying the legitimacy of another person or group. Self-will and self-interest would rule this moment in history when the sanctity of human life was proven to be worth far less than the need to pursue self-preservation.

Chapter One

THE NEW COMFORT ZONE

The moral argument has been made that human life begins at the time of inception. The argument has yet to be made that the credibility and relevance of that same human life, beyond the physical realm, begins at the time of learning the greatest gift he or she can possess during this lifetime are the inherent merits of character. Educate to build character and this moral argument is made.

Lorenzo D. Leonard

Branch Rickey, the Brooklyn Dodgers' baseball owner, made history with two bold steps. First, just prior to signing Jackie Robinson, the first African American ballplayer to compete in the American Major Leagues, and to play for his organization, Mr. Rickey said to him, "People aren't going to like this; they are going to do anything to get you to react. Echo a curse with a curse, and they will hear only yours. Follow a blow with a blow, and they will only see your blow. Your enemy will be out in force, and you cannot fight him on his territory." Mr. Robinson responded and said, "Do you want a player that doesn't have the guts to fight back?" Rickey then told the young ballplayer, "No, I want a player that has the guts not to fight back." The second bold historic step was to set before Jackie the opportunity to achieve success against the blatant display and treatment of racism. In order to achieve this success, Mr. Robinson would have to step a great distance outside of his comfort zone. Rather than to match power with power, anger with anger, hostility with hostility, and hatred with hatred, Jackie would need to develop and use qualities that represented honorable character.

Traits that would need to be personalized such as faith, trust, patience, humility, perseverance, accountability, vulnerability, transparency, empathy, forgiveness, and community would come to add multiple dimensions to Jackie as an individual. However, these additions would necessarily originate from an internal core of good that would confirm components of *who* Jackie was intrinsically. It is important to mention that Mr. Robinson's innate value had nothing in common or to do with *what* he was as a male African American ballplayer. What did factor into the overall picture was how the attributes of sound character coupled with his natural abilities to excel as a baseball player are what establishes Jackie as a credible pioneer of societal change. This profound success would subsequently open the doors for more African Americans, Latino ballplayers, and women to later cross the once-impenetrable race and gender barriers that existed throughout the sports world.

Mr. Robinson's willingness to confront his personal fears and step outside of his comfort zone is the point in time when success became inevitable. Without question, it would be much easier to remain attached to behavior weighed down with retaliation and resentment in reaction to racist acts that attempt to devalue and humiliate. As Mr. Rickey suggested, to rely on a comfort zone that would send a signal of an internalized racial inferiority through reactive measures would have short-circuited any possible success.

Branch Rickey knew that falling back into a comfort zone of

payback, indignation, hatred, anger, and violence was nothing more than resorting to power and control. Jackie would become one and the same as his oppressors and simply repeat common reactions to racial transgressions. To replicate impoverishment versus impoverishment would benefit no one, except the individual who labors under a victim mentality. Through a nonviolent and proactive approach, the demonstration of Mr. Robinson's merits of character was able to effectively neutralize and eventually diminish the evil influences and intimidation techniques of racism.

This was the same nonviolent and proactive approach to the perverted practices of racism that helped Mahatma Gandhi, the Reverend Martin Luther King Jr., Nelson Mandela, and their respective civil and human rights movements to experience success during their distinct periods in history. Stepping outside the comfort zone of overt reaction allowed the Indian, black South African, and African American to briefly interrupt the racial dominance, discrimination, and segregation practices that oppressed all three ethnic groups. However, despite such heroic accomplishments and many other such success stories, including Jackie Robinson's, the inability to lessen the evil within the world community derived from the institution of racism is quite evident.

The same can be said regarding the inability to lessen the evil originating from class and race warfare, ethnic cleansing, gender inequality, religious wars, and age discrimination. The prophetic words, "The more things change, the more they remain the same," become even more resounding as the value of a human life continues to diminish at the same time the human and civil rights of a person gain in token conversations. Such words that represent an obvious contradiction also give rise to the statement, "The evil of this world will continue to exist so long as it extends beyond humanity's belief that it can be destroyed."

The lack of success with diminishing the evils of racism within the world community can be traced to at least three fundamental reasons. First of all, mechanical respect, not credibility, and relevance were the actual accomplishments coming out of the previous historical civil and human rights struggles. For instance, though Mahatma Gandhi helped to achieve freedom from British rule for the Indians, Nelson Mandela broke the stranglehold of apartheid in South Africa, and the Reverend Martin Luther King Jr. led the march to desegregate schools and businesses for the African Americans, one reality remained a constant presence. Racism never diminished nor disappeared from the human experience. As a tool of oppression used to discredit and prove irrelevant the Indian, black South African, and African American, all three continue to remain victims of overt racism and participants who would victimize one another through covert racial practices.

A class system replaced British rule, an oppressive black government replaced white apartheid, and black-on-black oppression sat alongside white racism as a headline for depraved practices to demean and devalue. In other words, for all three ethnic groups, internalized racism has shared the stage with externalized racism The world community has responded to the cosmetic civil and human rights gains by establishing three new styles of communication when it comes to addressing one another: complete avoidance, political correctness, and respect with a deceptive smile—as opposed to a straightforward genuine acknowledgment of credibility. The difference between mechanical respect and credibility remains the large elephant in the living room no one wishes to address.

Educate to the merits of character and credibility replaces the ability to manipulate respect. Thus, a gathering of equals assures that the value of a human life is elevated above economic, racial, ethnic, gender, age, and religious relevance. It is the person that matters, and not *what* he or she represents externally. Social change resulting from civil and human rights initiatives were based on altering behavior toward an individual and group with a different background. Rather than learn to recognize the intrinsic value of a person where attitudes are truly changed and a new comfort zone initiated, symptomatic behavior became the focus, and the actual problem was ignored. In other words, emphasis was placed on changing the outward display of the problem and not the internal circumstance that created the problem in the first place. The Indian, black South African, African American, and their respective oppressors were unable to fully benefit from the example that made the Branch Rickey and Jackie Robinson nonviolent and proactive approach to racism so effective.

The nonviolent and proactive approach was also what made the black ballplayers that immediately followed Mr. Robinson into the American Major Leagues a huge success. None of these individuals, including Jackie Robinson, defined themselves by their experiences of abuse and discredit. Instead, these black pioneers chose to take the higher ground with their merits of character as the proactive response.

Larry Doby, the first African American to play for the Cleveland Indians, once stated, "I got a lot of resentment from a lot of teammates. But after a period of time they got an opportunity to judge me for who I was and not the color of my skin." He also stated, "I think that's one of the biggest things that happened in baseball, that we were able to integrate and judge for ourselves what kind of character these people had." Hank Thompson, Willard "Home Run" Brown, Monte Irvin, Sam "The Jet" Jethroe, Willie Mays, Bob Trice, Ernie Banks, Curt Roberts, and later, Hank Aaron and Roberto Clemente knew the importance of stepping outside of a comfort zone of reaction to embrace the personal qualities of humility, perseverance, and integrity.

Once an individual learns to identify and value his or her merits of character, this component of oneself becomes a natural link to credibility and relevant. Because this link to legitimacy is so natural, having its origin within the inner properties of an individual's personage, sustainability, is also an innate gift. This is not a fragile commodity that is here today, and suddenly, disappears tomorrow under the pressure of being called out as something other than credible. Strength of character provides an opportunity to neutralize the evil influences of racism or any form of oppressive behavior without internalizing and defining oneself by the experiences. Learning not to define oneself by his or her experiences is a huge benefit, which can be accredited to the development of the inherent gifts of strong character. Relying on the traits of good character to establish credibility and relevance allows a person to factor into him or her self-perception a personal worth that goes beyond the limiting borders of experiences, whether good or bad.

Credibility and relevance based on a personal demonstration of meritorious character was absent during earlier human and civil rights struggles that took place in India, South Africa, and America. Eliminating the practices of open discrimination and injustice toward a specific ethnicity and nationality were the areas that gained recognition for the Indian, black South African, and African American. Mahatma Gandhi, Nelson Mandela, and the Reverend Martin Luther King Jr. arose from their respective triumphs as saviors. However, the people with whom these three esteemed leaders represented had very little to hold onto except their ethnicity and nationality once their leaders were removed from the picture.

The short-term recognition and subsequent loss of moral purpose when leadership is no longer clearly defined or identified is quite common. This same phenomenon can be said to have occurred with many past historical struggles where the efforts to attain freedom and justice from an oppressive rule was primarily led by one individual. The issue has never been that the oppressed learn the value of substantive character; just that the oppressor stop with unjustly inflicting hardship, constraint, and abusive governance. Ethnic, religious, social, and cultural groups have long struggled with the issue of demanding freedom from oppression, but then resorting to oppressive behavior within and outside their respective ranks.

If this were not true, then it would not have been necessary for the Indian, black South African, and African American to become oppressive toward its own kind or to become one and the same as their respective tormentors. Within the African American community, violence, killing one another, and referring to each other as "my nigger" is permissible. But, when such acts are initiated against the community from outside, it is considered a racist undertaking. The South African Reconciliation Survey of 2012 compiled by Kate Lefko-Everett reports, "Eighteen years after the end of white minority rule, it found 43.5% of South Africans rarely or never speak to someone of another race. Little more than a quarter (27.4%) interact with a person of another race always or often on ordinary weekdays, while 25.9% do so sometimes." The survey goes on to say that "Less than one in five (17.8%) South Africans always or often socialize with people of other races in their homes or in the homes of friends. A further 21.6% do so sometimes, and more than half (56.6%) rarely or never socialize across race lines."[1]

Any behavior deficient in the recognition of credibility and relevance that supports the inherent sacredness of human life doubles as an act of repression, irrespective of the spin. Respect minus credibility is nothing more than an agent for deception. When attention is brought to the abuses and injustices due to racism, the focus is on eliminating the practices of degradation strictly for the individual or group considered the perpetrators. There is no question, relieving the

---

[1] Ticking Time Bomb or Demographic Dividend? Youth and Reconciliation in South Africa; South African Reconciliation Barometer Survey: 2012 Report; Kate Lefko-Everett; copyright 2012, Institute for Justice and Reconciliation; produced by COMPRESS.dsl.

Indian, black South African, and African American of the oppression flowing from the practice of racism was of paramount importance and extremely vital for humane reasons, alone. However, once again, lost in the discussion were the highly effective execution and methods used to neutralize the evil influences and intimidation methods of racism by the oppressed group.

The nonviolent and proactive approaches that comprised the strength of character would carry the brunt weight of change. Discovering a different and gratifying comfort zone through character development would have propelled the Indian, black South African, and African American to new heights of personal value and group unification. Rather than the usual internal distrust, envy, and suspicion, the aftereffects would have left all three groups with no need to internalize the experiences of racism, individually and collectively as a group. It would become unnecessary to continue referencing one another with terms and conditions that were a constant reminder of a past filled with persecution.

On the flip side of the coin, it wasn't necessary for the British, the white South African, or white American to learn such values of sound character. This simply was not to be, nor is it going to occur, so long as the three cultures are dominated and governed by a way of life that primarily associates the sanctity of human life with external and material value. The focus for change centered around the British, white apartheid, and white America stepping away from the practice of illegal dominance and abusive discriminatory practices. The distinction between respect and credibility was insignificant and immaterial; artificial and non-engaging respect would surely suffice. Polite respect would not have the white culture in Great Britain, South Africa, or America adopting a far-reaching new comfort zone.

Whereas, for the Indian, black South African, and African American to seek credibility, this expectation would have certainly pushed the envelope beyond what would be considered an acceptable reality. This would have been too far of a reach even for the Indian, black South African, and African American, as well. The focus on the value and development of the attributes of meritorious character had yet to arrive on the horizon for either three oppressed cultures. In addition, it makes for a perfect contradiction to seek credibility and relevance from external sources, and this acknowledgment has not taken place on an internal basis.

Though this may have been the case, it was still necessary for the Indian, black South African, and African American to learn such values as credibility and relevance if these ethnic groups were to move beyond the practice of racism. It did not matter if the appearance of racism was internalized or externally displayed toward other groups of people. If these groups were to move beyond their respective oppressors, an education to substantive character would be a prerequisite. But, as is the situation with past and current human and civil rights struggles, the maltreated can only accomplish this feat if there is a willingness to separate from a need to serve the same way of life as the tyrant. And that particular way of life has to do with attaching the greatest value of an individual to *what* he or she is externally and possesses materially. The sacredness of human life can only be appreciated when an individual understands the greatest value he or she brings to this existence is the inherent gifts of substantive character.

To be good and to do good does not require perfection, but it does require a willingness to step out of one's comfort zone of familiarity. This applies to the person experiencing credibility and authority solely based on *what* he or she is externally. And the person lacking in external importance and relevance does not measure up to external standards is also charged with stepping outside his or her comfort zone of familiarity. Though some measure of authority and token respect is derived from living on either side of the equation, it is the sense of power and esteem that are the major reasons why people are so reluctant to step outside of a zone of comfort . . . be it good or bad. Again, both sides of this socioeconomic equation serve a way of life that principally values *what* an individual is externally and possesses materially. To be good and to do good requires that a person learn to create a new zone of comfort where credibility and relevance make no distinction with respect to economics, class, gender, race, ethnicity, family, education, and religion.

Judgments made as to the importance or lack of importance based on external circumstances make it virtually impossible to be good and to do good without conditions dictating motivation. It makes no difference; impoverished thought afflicts both sides of the relevant and irrelevant equation, because each is deficient in an education to the personal merits of character. Each possesses an insufficient understanding as to the best human component to his or her existence. Therefore, the rich, poor, and middle will seek to benefit through a process of manipulation, either the elevation or collapse of his or her credibility and relevance.

As long as a person's well-being is sought solely through external sources, self-importance will rise and fall due to self-indulgence. The reluctance to step outside of his or her comfort zone to experience an unfamiliar approach to personal development and growth also has to do with living out a strongly held custom. The norm is to support a way of life that flourishes and exists based on faulty information. Where the value of external and material success supersedes the value and effectiveness of the attributes of good character, a flawed training overshadows the human existence. The invalid information arising from such training reinforces the idea that the best way to define one's self in either an inflated or deflated manner is by his or her experiences.[2]

Credibility and relevance, or their lack, form a self-perception

---

[2] To define one's self strictly by personal experiences that are either good, bad, or indifferent are explained in more detail in Chapter 3.

solely based on experiences, which is incorrect. If an individual is not taught that he or she is more than experiences alone, how is that same person to know that he or she is more than the good, bad, and indifferent experiences being encountered on a daily basis? Lost in the development process is the understanding that the personal defining process also includes his or her attributes of good character. The idea that "something is better than nothing"[3] plays a huge role in hanging onto a state of physical and emotional ease inside the cocoon often referred to as the zone of comfort and familiarity.

Nevertheless, there is zero opportunity to learn about one's self and others when situated inside a cocoon offering simplicity and limitations. The sky's the ceiling for learning and reaching his or her full potential as a person with sustainable meaning and purpose. Standing outside, the familiar with the merits of character as tools for personal discovery, development, and practical options for redemption when mistakes do occur allow for accountability, transparency, and vulnerability to work wonders.

As long as humanity fails to make a genuine effort to establish an educational curriculum that speaks to the value and development of a person's merits of character, where the true value of an individual is derived, a stark prediction gains momentum. Putting it more exactly, the words of George F. Kennan, former United States Ambassador to the Soviet Union from May 14, 1952–September 19, 1952, become a prophecy. Kennan stated, "We should cease to talk about vague and unreal objectives such as human rights, the raising of the living standards, and democratization. The day is not far off when we are going to have to deal in straight power concepts. The less we are then hampered by idealistic slogans, the better."

The day is no longer far off, for humanity is now fully engaged in

---

[3] The statement "something is better than nothing" is explored in more detail in Chapter 3.

nothing but a rapture of straight power concepts. As the overall worth of a human life continues to dramatically decline in terms of credibility and relevance, the global community stands by besieged by rhetoric of domination and persuasive non-apologetic justifications—from dictators representing large and small dominions, extremist groups representing distorted and perverted religious ideology, to mass killings and genocide by despairing individuals perpetuating fear and violence. The end result is to feel what amounts to a distorted and depraved sense of relevance.

The following is a comprehensive treatise pertaining to the sanctity of human life. The time has arrived to look past getting behind leaders who mistakenly do the work that is long overdue for the masses to accomplish. No longer is it in the best interest of the people to develop an unhealthy dependency on the countless heroes and heroines who step away from their respective comfort zones and make personal sacrifices to advance humanity beyond impoverished living conditions. Mahatma Gandhi, the Reverend Martin Luther King Jr., Nelson Mandela, Jackie Robinson, and a multitude of men and women throughout history have sacrificed their lives to help advance humanity beyond emotional, intellectual, and spiritual impoverishment to a more civilized and moral responsible existence. The personal sacrifices and achievements of all these individuals, as well as those to come, cannot be overlooked nor minimized.

However, this form of reliance seduces the assembly into avoiding an important personal life lesson. To learn on a personal level, the process that teaches how and where the sacredness of human life is derived remains the most important life lesson to date. The individual learning process continues to be the development of a person's merits of character. The time has arrived to look toward establishing a gathering of equals willing to exemplify leadership skills by developing his or her strengths of character. To value the sacredness of human life requires learning to recognize and appreciate the essence of honorable character. And once the merits of character are valued to the same extent, or more, with respect to *what* an individual is externally and possesses materially, personal experiences will no longer be accepted as the sole means to define a person.

Stepping outside the personal comfort zone provided by class, race, ethnicity, religion, gender, politics, and age to embrace the genuine elements of the human existence, which is his or her strengths of character, replaces impoverishment with empowerment. What is known up to this point in time is that unchecked power and domination left to advance an agenda motivated by self-importance and self-indulgence produces one certainty. The misrepresentation of the true application of authority by means of misuse and abuse is always the end result. To pursue credibility and legitimacy by demeaning and manipulating the principle of integrity to satisfy self-interest undermines the cohesive element of any community.

World history is saturated with example after example of the shameless and brazen use of authority to pursue credibility and legitimacy that disavows the sacredness of human life. The pursuit of superiority and dominance continues to divide humanity well into the twenty-first century. This, at the same time a continuous procession marches on toward glorious cemeteries, monuments, and the bestowing of accolades for its victims of naïveté. And to this present date in history, humankind has yet to learn that such indefensible pursuits are the results of a continuous and distressing human condition directly related to an uncontested state of emotional and spiritual impoverishment.[4]

No, it is not human nature to devour its own kind, as conventional

---

[4] *Empires vs. Coalitions: A Defining Moment for Relationships*; Lorenzo D. Leonard; published by Strategic Book Publishing and Rights Co., Houston, Texas, 2013; page 155-162.

wisdom would suggest. It is a condition of impoverishment that has taught humanity to betray humanity. As a consequence of not being challenged by an education of substantive and meritorious character, humanity keeps alive an old proverb: "The evil of this world will continue to exist so long as it extends beyond humanity's belief that it can be destroyed." This disconcerting condition has had such a negative impact upon humankind to the extent that the act of self-betrayal impedes this same humanity from fulfilling its moral obligation. First in line regarding this responsibility is the individual, and second to one another as a civilization. And that moral commitment, whether accepted or not, is to help improve and elevate the human experience: regardless of race, gender, religion, age, and material differences. The consequence that persistently follows the misuse of authority is how unchecked power and domination become a principal detriment to understanding the value of the sacredness of human life, both for the community and purveyor.

Once it is understood how and where the proper use of authority is actually developed, the sacredness of human life will rise in value and elevated meaning. And once it is understood that the honorable use of authority has nothing to do with status, position, neither credentials, nor power covertly or overtly granted through tradition, evil is diminished. Human life is advanced to a meaning that will not be lessened by any effort on the part of unabated power and control to weaken its worth and effectiveness. It is important to understand that an individual cannot and will not be in a position to fulfill his or her moral responsibility until there is acceptance of his or her merits of character; the inherent gift each and every human embodies.

It can take a lifetime to fully grasp and appreciate the sanctity of human life. It can also take this same lifetime to fully understand and demonstrate that no human endeavor will ever displace the sacredness of human life in terms of credence and importance. Again, even though conventional wisdom would attempt to convey a different idea with its enticement that power and material gain supersede the virtue of human life in terms of absolute deference, this is simply seductive thinking lacking any moral fortitude. The reason why it takes a lifetime to value and demonstrate sanctity for human life is that it takes that length of time to dismantle and disavow the erroneous teachings that support an opposite viewpoint.

It also takes a lifetime to fully understand that one cannot approach a true appreciation of the nobility of human life while holding onto a belief that the personal glass is half-empty or half-full based on external and material value or its deficiency. When employing the narcissistic weapon of comparison, the sacredness of human life can never be genuinely appreciated. This simply cannot take place while holding onto the belief that one is less than or more than with respect to another person: regardless of external and material ranking. Developing an appreciation for the decency of human life will always begin with recognizing and developing an appreciation for one's own life, which will begin with the basics of one's life: the merits of character.

To cherish and meticulously protect the newborn and lavish this infant with the gift of sacredness is a superb parenting skill. But, to painstakingly await that magical moment when the infant is of an age to be methodically instructed on the various societal and cultural means made available to gain an upper hand over a faction of humanity considered inferior is an erroneous teaching of great proportion. The reverse instruction can also be true for the young and innocent to experience. To be methodically taught of the different societal and cultural means that will devalue the up and coming as incompetent and deficient is once again an erroneous teaching of a huge proportion.

Humankind bears responsibility for an educational system that short circuits the opportunity to learn about the attributes of mutuality and equality, which begin with learning about his or her strengths of character. The comfort zone of class, race, ethnicity, gender, religion, and politics are just a few of many societal and cultural packages of bias that await the arrival of the age-appropriate child. The sanctity of human life will begin to meld into an individual's life when it is understood that no matter *what* an individual is externally and materially, that person will always be part of a larger community: the human race. And as a fundamental part of this acceptance, there is recognition of the moral responsibility that each member of this community has to one another. To improve and elevate the human experience through the execution of a committed effort to educate and demonstrate the value and effectiveness of substantive character is the central core of that moral responsibility.

The young and innocent are routinely conditioned to view that a person or persons different from themselves, individually or as a group, as probable adversaries when the issue of credibility and relevance are being discovered. Advocates for associating power with credibility know all too well how to project and define an adversary based on class, race, ethnicity, gender, and religious differences. The deliberate attempt to declare measurements of superiority and inferiority based on *what* an individual is externally and possesses materially is the starting point. Rather than use that magical teaching moment to instruct the impressionable and young on the importance of embracing and demonstrating attributes of good character, such as equality, mutuality, credibility, generosity, and integrity, an unfortunate turn of events occur.

The sacredness of human life is unceremoniously laid to rest in favor of resurrecting the insensible teachings regarding the benefits of exploitation through self-importance and self-indulgence. *What* an individual is externally and materially is taught to be of a greater value and enormity than *who* that individual is intrinsically with respect to the merits and substance of character. It is extremely problematic to convey and teach any individual, young or adult, the value regarding the sacredness of human life when the exploits of self-importance and self-indulgence are given greater deference. And its consequence, the use of authority becomes a dictate and command, rather than mutually and respectfully measured.

A custom closely adhered to, one that encourages genuine discourse regarding the sacredness of human life, routinely takes place after the passing of an important personality or the loss of life due to a natural or human-made disaster. For example, when a suicide or terrorist bomb explodes, killing and injuring scores of people, or when a destructive hurricane, tornado, flood, earthquake, forest fire, coal mine implosion, or oil spill takes place, there is customarily honest conversation, grief, and community that shortly follows regarding the importance of human life. Eventually, the short-lived compassion subsides, and it is back to the business of maintaining dissenting groups. Very little discourse or attempts are ever made on an international or national level to address the need to improve the human existence and fellowship among its living participants outside of a natural or human-made disaster.

The time has arrived to set aside nationalistic, political, economic, or religious differences, as well as race, ethnic, and gender differences to have a series of genuine conversations about community building. The sacredness of human life deserves the effort to improve and elevate this earthly existence. Throughout the ages, men and women have labored under the naïve notion that one way to protect humanity from vigorously and viciously exploiting its own in a negative manner is to legislate morality. The rule of law has been thought to be an immense guardian toward protecting humanity from itself. By itself, without addressing the state of impoverishment that immorally grips the human race along with its antidote, makes such efforts just another exercise in a recycling process.

Educating the masses to the merits of character will change the hearts and minds of people, which, in turn, will weaken and reduce the impact of impoverishment with empowerment. There is no question the previous statement can come across to the reader as romanticized and extremely optimistic. This statement, as it stands, certainly makes educating the masses to the merits of character sound like an easy process to undertake. It also goes without saying that people cannot change overnight, for this particular endeavor is a slow and methodical development. Still, the effort has to be made to provide some people with developing a system of living that supports the sanctity of human life. And, while we should still try to drag the masses from upholding a corrupt system of living, some people will continue to pursue power and domination.

To legislate morality without educating the masses to recognize, value, and demonstrate the moral attributes that also can protect humanity from victimizing itself with impoverished thinking is parallel to the illogical. This lone gesture is akin to washing the body without the assistance of soap with the expectation to cleanse the physical structure. The sacredness of human life has, time after time, been disregarded to the unforgiving behavior of self-importance and self-indulgence. The rule of law, coupled with the merits of character, can guarantee an end to this historically based practice.

An agenda often revealed during efforts to protest against abuse and misuse of authority that are, by design, in support of the sacredness of human life, but are engaged in behavior that mimics the injustice, are simply at cross-purposes. No rebellion that demonstrates antisocial behavior can ever be effective when impersonating the oppression. Bring forth from within what separates the person or group from the oppression and oppressor, and a new comfort zone is created through the process of defining one's self by the merits of his or her character. When civilization begins in earnest to teach that to stay within the confines of one's inherent authority that represent the attributes of good character, a person will have no need to overstep his or her authority to feel relevant. Absent an educational system that encourages a person to recognize, value, and practice his or her inherent qualities of good character, and one phenomena is a historical certainty.

Learning how to motivate people to develop contempt for one another based on obvious and shallow external differences is a simple task to accomplish. All that is required is to equate credibility and relevancy with power, supremacy, and prominence. The inability to live one's life based on the good qualities of his or her character is consistently confirmed by an impulse to follow the judgments, teachings, and dictates from external sources. The problem that arises from such choices is the lack of interest expressed by the external sources in establishing a relationship based on reciprocal rights and duties. The inability to live one's life established on his or her strengths of character is always a precursor for the type of relationships to follow. The tendency to be exploited due to a willingness to accept, without questioning, the framework on which relationships will pivot produces one result. Over a period of time, relationships based on the accommodation and performance model generate a great deal of anguish and resentment due to the lack of mutuality.

So long as the pain associated with a need to be credible and relevant is dampened somewhat, conditional acceptance from any relationship will suffice. To remain distrusting of the stability his or her merits of character can provide for individuality makes it is easy for disinterested external sources, such as race, ethnicity, and religion, to define a person in either an inflated or deflated manner. There is no resistance to the tactics used, since there is no understanding on that individual's part regarding where and how his or her true value is derived. The knowing and unknowing personal sacrifices made to external sources that presume positions of superiority or inferiority in the end offer nothing more than betrayal and abandonment. The personal sacrifices made in order to achieve a distorted sense of credibility or irrelevance can never nor will ever quench the thirst and hunger for the genuine. The time has more than arrived to step into a new comfort zone where betrayal, abandonment, and disappointment are vastly diminished.

As a consequence, to living like ships passing at night, a person will often yearn to experience distinction and affection that is lacking in relationships founded on utilitarian purpose, which, by its very nature, is conditional. To cope with such a desire while being consumed with the drive to achieve external and material value, the attempt is made to simultaneously use its intensity to quiet the internal appetite. It seems like a natural circumstance to undertake without appearing wanting. It is not uncommon to move from one day to the next with an endeavor to balance the holy war that is stirring within the interior. The internal desire to experience that which is authentic and the need to satisfy external expectations based on accommodation and performance can be unsettling. Whether or not to trust the appearance relationships may portray, especially when deception is an integral part of a system structured on accommodation and performance, can be a source of anxiety.

Nonetheless, though quite genuine, the yearning must remain as such due to a need to maintain a level of hope the current condition of bliss does not melt away. It is understandable as to the origin of anguish when bliss does appear to be melting away. Educate a woman, man, and child to his or her gifts of character and there will always be room at a table other than where the powerful and prominent hold court. It does not matter what the physical characteristics may consist of or what the material portfolio may hold or not. Because the qualities of substantive character are limitless, no table is too small, no ladder too short. The beauty of discovering and putting into practice his or her inherent gifts of character are the special moments that witness bringing forth a personal wealth of talent. More importantly, an individual has the opportunity to pursue with success a life's journey of personally defining *who* he or she is as revealed through the recognition of the qualities of character.

This process is more substantial and meaningful than simply settling to be defined by outside sources, titles, and labels either measuring up to or down to a value system least interested in a priceless humanity. *What* an individual is externally and possesses materially can always be of value today and tomorrow have zero value. Thus, with this way of life and its exaggerated importance on the accumulation of power and prominence for levitating self-worth, credibility and relevancy are consistently at risk of vaporizing. Not so when the *who* factor is the stabilizing foundation of an individual's life, where character development can never be stripped, downsized, or even sold.

Integrity and credibility, which are the attributes of good character that provide assurance to the cohesion of any community, are easily ignored and dismissed when authority takes on the presentation of a dictate and command. Under such conditions, the sanctity of human life is reduced to a mere abstract idea. To marginalize and deem irrelevant a human life, because that person or group does not measure up to predetermined standards that are exclusive of the merits of character, cripples the moral development of all human life. This crippling act affects both the judge and the judged. Religious conflicts and wars, world wars, international and domestic civil conflicts and terrorism, unregulated capitalism, oppressive communism, and repressive socialism have, throughout humanity's history, remained consistent with one common theme.

The retelling of the same exhausting story of a total disregard for the sacredness of human life has long pasted any form of usefulness to humankind. In conjunction with the usual human creations of classism, racism, sexism, and religious superiority, humanity continues to recycle one consistent historical commentary: "the more things change, the more they remain the same." This, all in the name of self-interest as it is staged through efforts to manipulate power and prominence. Impoverishment continues to impede civilization from fulfilling its most important and immediate mission, which is to help elevate and improve the human experience. A practical approach to accomplishing this responsibility remains through the education and demonstration of meritorious character, which is a natural safeguard for protecting the sacredness of its existence.

Chapter Two

CREDIBILITY AND RELEVANCE

"I Have A Dream"

"I say to you today, my friends, so even though we face the difficulties of today and tomorrow, I still have a dream. It is a dream deeply rooted in the American dream. I have a dream that one day this nation will rise up and live out the true meaning of its creed: We hold these truths to be self-evident that all men are created equal. I have a dream that my four little children will one day live in a nation where they will not be judged by the color of their skin but by the content of their character. I have a dream today."

Martin Luther King Jr., 1963, in Washington, D.C.

The question: Well, who are you?

Response: No one, and that is as we go, thus we become.

Game of Thrones S5 E3

Unless a person is a closeted or openly self-proclaimed autocrat, it is rather safe to make the following assumption: For an unspecified number of individuals, beginning his or her day with the goal to be good and to do good is a personal ambition, to be taken seriously. To be a virtuous neighbor to individuals that he or she would intersect with is all that matters, irrespective of economic, racial, ethnic, religious, educational, and political differences.

Contrary to the world's track record regarding despicable reactions when differences are discovered, giving meaning to "we live at peace with each other, which is good" is the specific intention. Living outside an ill-conceived sense of immunity from repercussions stemming from absolute rule permits such a serious contemplation. Energized by a need to feel cooperative, and spurred on by honorable intentions, the daily goal for these individuals dramatically differs from that of the autocrat. It is no secret; the leading daily goal for any absolute ruler has always been and will continue to be how to achieve more dominance, authority, and prestige.

This agenda is slightly different from the person or group living outside the ill-advised developed sense of immunity from consequences of the total power to mandate. For credibility purposes, a primary goal set forth by this faction is to simply hold on to economic, racial, ethnic, political, social, and religious advantages established through longstanding inequalities and inequities. Having been in existence for what seems like the beginning of time, the unfair practices have become rationalized away as nothing more than the cost of existing in a less-than-perfect system of living. As witnessed through the eyes of history, such practices were once explicit and boldly carried out. Through the eyes of modern-day history, income disparities, racial injustice, gender bias, ethnic and age prejudice, religious intolerance, education dissimilarities, domestic violence, and child abuse continue to dominate the overall human landscape.

While the narrative has essentially remained unchanged,

inequalities and inequities have shifted from an overt to a covert format. The cruel and insensitive elements attached to the practice of inequities have forced a change to occur in terms of an open display of contempt to a subtler and sophisticated format. Though the practice of racial, ethnic, gender, and age intolerance is as lethal as ever, these forms of discrimination have become progressively more difficult to prove. It is not fashionable to be associated with the evil emerging from the practice of injustice. Every effort is made to avoid being linked to creating hell in another's person's life; yet, the injustice continues unabated.

A system of living that attaches the primary form of credibility to the external and material also installs inequalities and inequities as natural elements to create an illusion of security. It is for this reason that discrimination and injustice are here to stay; that is, until character development is finally made a fundamental part of the educational process. A hands-off or head-in-the-sand approach to the practice of inequalities and inequities simply are not acceptable responses to offenses against the superiority of ethics. Neither are statements like, "I was not there when acts of discrimination and injustice were originally executed," and "I have nothing to do with modern-day acts of bigotry and unfairness." Such self-serving declarations are absent of validity when put forth as reasons to discharge oneself of any personal responsibility.

There are no defensible reasons that exonerate a person while he or she benefits from the economic, social, racial, gender, educational, and religious injustice that create imbalances to elevate one faction of humanity and relegate another faction as irrelevant. But, this is to be expected from a system of living that glorifies the external and material, and, at the same time, ignores the intrinsic nature and value of substantive character. Doing nothing to eradicate the demeaning practice of discrimination and injustice, which includes sitting on the cushioned sidelines providing mere lip service in opposition, begs the question as to the overall sincerity of the morning ambition.

Though surface goals may differ for the self-confessed autocrat and authoritarian, do not overlook the fact that at the end of the day, both factions enjoy a way of life that is quite the same below the exterior. For example, the status quo lives on with inequities and inequalities surviving as dominant contributors to a divisive and imbalanced system of living. If apathy and indifference continue, very little, if any, will change on a personal level to initiate neutralizing a system of living riddled with discrimination and injustice. Due to a lack of real effort on an individual level, the dial representing change does not move one decimal on a collective basis. This is not to say that the type of change necessary to awaken an individual to his or her true value and credibility is absent from the personal development theater.

On the contrary, there are numerous individuals exhibiting the courage and willingness to learn and put into play the merits of his or her character. This grouping of individuals who are willing to live life based on his or her inherent good represent excellent examples for character development. Rather than invest in a system punctured with pseudo and conditional standards posing as sustainable good, these individuals choose to respond to what is considered the highest calling any person can answer to within this life cycle. Answering the call to honor the intrinsic nature and value of meritorious character allows a person to interface with his or her neighbor or the stranger on a genuine and ethical level, irrespective of economic, racial, ethnic, political, gender, age, and religious differences. This is made possible due to having come to understand that his or her true value is in principle based on an internal legitimacy, rather than the unsustainable external and material.

The commitment to engage with coalitions or groups of equals are regarded as worthy and viable endeavors. Time is viewed as an invaluable asset, not to be wasted with deceptive conversations and actions. That given as a way of life, the individual subjectively pledges to say what he or she actually means and intends to convey. In addition to this viewpoint is the pledge to honor the credibility, not only as it pertains to him or herself, but to the individual or group on the other side of the conversation. This is a vital lesson to learn if a person is to avoid being confused or deceived about what is true or untrue. It is difficult to know what is true or real when so much time is devoted to saying the opposite of what a person means and wants to convey. What he or she would like to honestly convey is silenced by the mute button for fear of being too vulnerable and transparent when disclosing information that is of a personal nature.

Vulnerability and transparency are two character traits frowned upon and discouraged within a system of living that promotes the development of power and the need to be right over the value of ethical behavior. However, it is interesting to note that the thought process is never hindered by the fear of being vulnerable and transparent while seeking to damage or destroy the credibility of another person or group. When the effort is made to seek or advance personal credibility by taking apart such fundamental elements for another person, such as relevance and legitimacy, the peddler of such tactics has failed to learn a critical life lesson.

First of all, disparaging criticism, contemptible condemnation, or outright character assassination are tools of the weak. Second, vulnerability and transparency used for purposes other than their intended use, which are to reveal the depth of worthy character and not its opposite, provide disappointing results. Unbeknownst to the purveyor, the person ends up tarnishing and oftentimes destroys his or her credibility during the process. Magnified within a system of living that solely honors power and domination is how difficult it is to learn this lesson, let alone to be open for an exchange of ideas regarding the subject matter. The institutions of religion, politics, and government immediately come to mind as examples where unbridled attacks on the credibility of another person or group are sanctioned.

On a more noteworthy side, an individual who is committed to answering the call to honor the intrinsic nature and value of meritorious character is also devoted to going the extra mile with expanding his or her traits of good character. The person is willing to provide for others what he or she would like to receive from others, rather than expect or demand what he or she refuses to give to others. Yes, mistakes will occur within the theater of relationships. Miscalculation of judgment, misunderstandings, and failures will occur on this human plane. However, what regularly will follow in order to learn and correct future experiences are the properties linked with integrity: accountability, mutual consideration, and personal responsibility.

What makes it possible to lean into introspective thought to learn from conflict is the education to commendable character. The ability to define one's self by the traits of good character, rather than solely by experiences, pays dividends in terms of developing an accurate assessment of his or her value. As fortune would have it, this way of life is overshadowed by a system of living that solely equates relevance and credibility with *what* a person has achieved externally and possesses materially. In the judgment of this particular system, this is answering the highest calling a person can respond to in this life cycle.

With one option available to define individual value, it is easy to predict the repercussion when the lone measuring gauge to reach this determination is through his or her experiences. A person either arrives at feeling as a failure, inconsequential, and unworthy, or he or she arrives at feeling as a model of success, consequential, and worthy. To internalize either personal view purely based on experiences, which are subsequently used to inflate or deflate importance, constitutes a misleading characterization of his or her self. Personal evaluations of one's self minus the recognition and value of his or her merits of character can develop into distorted and often perverted creations. Just as telling is the vigilance required to refrain from adopting a personal relevance or irrelevance pertaining to rulings that arise from external sources.

Societal customs, cultural traditions, and religious decrees often offer mandates that make relevance and irrelevance primarily based on *what* a person is externally, and this judgment includes material possessions. Importance and authority linked with presumed economic, race, ethnic, gender, and religious superiority creates an exaggerated sense of credibility. Conversely, with no special or distinctive features, *what* an individual is plays a major role in assessing degrees of less importance and irrelevance. This is a natural consequence when standing firm with the pursuit to seek relevance within a way of life that rigidly establishes credibility based on material and external value. Both perceptions with respect to relevance and irrelevance are made easily accessible for any person who is willing to allow personal value to be strictly determined through his or her experiences.

The personal cost associated with accepting either flawed self-perception is a relinquishing of the ability to question, probe, or elicit information from a position of strength. The capacity to do so demonstrates an individual's trust in his or her innate relevance and resources, which is a confirmation of character development. Such a personal endorsement constitutes an acceptance and understanding regarding the reliability of his or her inherent credibility. This affirmation also indicates an awareness that reveals inherent credibility to be a viable and authentic component originating within the individual. Otherwise, a person is left to develop a primary and unreliable dependence on another person's perception of relevance, resources, or even doctrine where measuring up is a distant carrot.

It is always a wiser endeavor to rely upon one's own innate legitimacy where measuring up is never brought into question. In the final analysis, such an undertaking is a much more practical method with sustainable results in which to achieve credibility. To seek relevance from external sources accomplishes nothing, except to create a relationship of disparity with respect to influence and management. Without fail, an allegiance of this nature is a dangerous precedent to initiate. Any relationship where there is a handing over to a person, group, or doctrine the responsibility and power to define relevance or irrelevance immediately creates a foundation severely impaired by inequality and inequity.

To adopt a personal view as being relevant or irrelevant based strictly on the external evaluations derived from traditions, customs, or doctrines conveys an acceptance of the notion that individual empowerment has little to no value, reality, or factual basis. What develops as a result of this surrender is a mannerism that basically is reflective of an overall lack of experience, wisdom, or judgment. And this mannerism is mostly revealed when engaged with an individual or group advocating for a way of life based on absolute authority, superiority, and compliance. Again, this posture of "going along to get along" necessitates foregoing the opportunity to exercise the personal authority of questioning individuals or doctrine as to the ethical and moral validity of empire building.

In many interpersonal circles, a designated subordinate cannot question a person or group representing power and authority for fear of punishment. Because the education, development, and value of substantive character is lacking, an even more demanding price is extracted from the person adapting his or her self-perception to experiences. The pathway to resolving conflict, whether personal or interpersonal, is thought to be rectified by creating more conflict, which only inflames the issue of conflict. The development of the merits of character allow for conflict to be resolved through measures allied with personal empowerment, not through the execution of power, deception, and vengeance.

It is not surprising to learn that a way of life preoccupied with obtaining importance and value attached to *what* an individual is externally and possesses materially is just as absorbed with another personal quest. Every waking hour is devoted to satisfying a very basic human instinct, which is to feel relevant. Though unsustainable and difficult to maintain at a consistent level, a prevailing thought remains solid: feel relevant through any external means necessary to ensure a level of mental health. Under such a predisposition, it is also understanding how the unjust and intolerant treatment of different categories of people becomes an inevitable evil to inhabit the human landscape. To protect the status of his or her relevance and guard against any perceived external threat that could lessen that ranking is its principal duty. And evil will exist in this world so long as it exceeds the belief that it can be destroyed.

For this reason, inequity and inequality arising from class, race, gender, ethnic, religious, and age discrimination simply will never disappear from the human landscape. It is naïve and foolish to believe otherwise, as long as the education and development of honorable character continues to remain absent from this landscape. To achieve relevance, and thus, credibility, it is normal to employ components of self-importance and self-indulgence, which fit perfectly within a way of life that equates prominence with power. One element that helps to establish dominance and relevance in a fairly deceptive manner is the strategy to seek or demand from others what he or she refuses to give to others. In response to the rallying cry of "team," support, reverence, and importance consistently are directed toward the specified relevant person due to a covert expectation to do so or an overt request.

Provided by the esteemed relevant individual are token gestures of importance to persons deemed of lesser significance, but who contribute some form of utility to the relationship. Another strategy is to engage in discussions and enterprises for the purpose of advancing a personal agenda primarily focused on being right. To gain or acquire new information or facts is of little to no importance. Discussions and enterprises offer a chance to partake in self-indulgence and self-absorption, which is a quick and easy method for experiencing personal relevance Exchanging ideas for the purpose of understanding or creating ventures for altruistic reasons simply are not in the equation for establishing credibility and relevance.

The motivation to create customs, traditions, rituals, and mores formed on a basis of superiority and unfairness are actually derived from a genuine instinct to feel relevant and worthy. However, as a result of built-in inequities and inequalities, individuals and groups are often targeted to inherit its adverse effects. Women, the poor and elderly, various racial, and ethnic groups across the human spectrum become casualties of differing institutions that equate power with relevance. Religious, marital, legal, educational, and health-care establishments are leading candidates. Hence, the continuous effort to elevate and simultaneously discredit on the basis of national, economic, gender, racial, ethnic, religious, social, and educational differences to assert relevance. Power and authority dictate which side of the dissimilarity is determined to be relevant, and which side is less consequential. In reality, what is actually motivated by a legitimate instinct unfortunately becomes linked with distortion and frequently, the perverted.

Major divisions of humankind continue to clash among one another to determine which is more pertinent and superior to the other. Various nations, religions, social classes, racial types, and ethnic groups engage in barbaric fights and struggles not only within their own borders, but well outside their boundaries for one purpose. And that solitary purpose is to prove relevance and credibility through power and dominance in whatever manner this agenda will take shape. Along with being victorious is an expectation the opposition will accept the idea of being irrelevant and inconsequential. It is indisputable when it comes to governing: the psychologically, emotionally, and spiritually defeated are willing and easy to be controlled. Based on inflated self-perceptions and standards that elevate hypocrisy to a divine principle, humanity continues to undermine its fundamental right to exist as a sovereign entity. Primarily due to its irreverence to character development, this basic right remains just an abstract idea. Humankind's refusal to embrace this inherent authority based on the gifts of character preserves the abstract, instead of an actuality.

Inequities and inequalities that prohibit by law, rule, or other directives, any segment of humanity to live his or her life in an unrestricted and unlimited manner essentially impedes every segment of the human race from achieving this privilege. The push to attain relevance and credibility under conditions that foster classism, sexism, racism, and religious power elites will necessarily force power and dominance to protect inequities and inequalities. For the same reason the addict will need to keep increasing his or her drug to achieve a state of bliss, so will power and dominance need to keep feeding its lack of freedom for the euphoria attached to a control-driven relevance.

Inequities and inequalities when threatened with extinction will become more and more subtle to detect. Hence, an argument for the continuation of classism, sexism, racism, adultism, and religious oligarchies, which all provide an effortless pathway to relevance and credibility. The absence of integrity at the intersection of human engagement guarantees this result. Such a void will expose how power and dominance are used to safeguard injustice and mask discrimination.

Despite social, political, and religious insistence to suggest otherwise, a historical and modern-day theme continues to reveal a glaring limitation to the formal educational process. Learning the fundamental curriculums that are necessary for a person to effectively function within his or her society is the correct educational endeavor to mandate. To enter into a system of living primarily focused on declaring credibility based on *what* an individual is externally and possesses materially necessitates such a decree. However, when the actual education, value, and development of the qualities linked to good character are absent from this educational format, the result is clear. Qualities of meritorious character such as integrity, account-ability, and transparency are not stressed as invaluable to the moral growth and development of the individual.

Developing such qualities help to make clear *who* an individual is with respect to his or her inherent value, which provides more mean-ing and sustainability to credibility. Instead, what is taken away from this one-tract system of learning is an evolution of intellectual, emo-tional, and spiritual dependency on external sources for relevance and credibility. Under this limited system of learning, a person is trained to always be prepared and expected to prove personal value if he or she is desirous of achieving relevance. Empathy and compas-sion are reserved for that person unable to measure up to standards and expectations in the attempt to achieve relevance and credibility. Great effort is often exerted toward an individual or group with the hope of attaining some measure of importance, only to be rejected time and time again.

The understanding that can frequently go unnoticed when pursu-ing legitimacy from external sources is that no amount of effort will ever be enough to warrant recognition. With a way of life predicated on power, authority, and prestige, sharing the stage or spotlight with a person or group considered of a lesser status is out of the question. Coupled with defining personal value or its lack through experiences, and a void of instructions regarding character development, the effect is predictable. The accumulation of experiences culminating in false positives or false negatives can prove to be misleading regarding self-perception.

Establish a system of learning with its focus on character develop-ment parallel to the formal educational system, and the effect is also predictable. To no one's surprise, the upshot will be training people to launch his or her life from a more balanced perspective with respect to achieving relevance and credibility. Relying just as thoughtfully on inherent value as he or she would with external and material attributes will create an accurate self-perception. Preciseness is assured, because there is an absence of the props of class, gender, race, ethnicity, and religion for purposes of identification. An individual learns to live his or her life based on the good attributes of character, not on the low-hanging fruit cultivated by inequities and inequalities.

Tradition, customs, and doctrines that support either false positives or false negatives with respect to self-perception can finally be seen as nothing more than distractions from a distinct truism. A person can refuse the need to feel depressed, anxiety-ridden, angry, neurotic, or psychotic, because he or she cannot measure up to standards that ignore the recognition of inherent value. The understanding that relevance and credibility are the result of a well-founded and sustainable self-perception refined by the attributes of good character is a welcomed revelation. Once the qualities of good character are accepted as legitimate and valuable components to a his or her total existence, there is no need to use the weapon of comparison to remind one's self of what he or she lacks in the external and material world. This being the case, depression, anxiety and anguish maintain limited roles in his or her life.

Rather than devote his or her life proving personal value with uncertain responses to follow, the outcome is not up in the air when relevance and credibility are derived through the merits of character. The need to develop a dependency on external sources passing its blessings or not as to his or her relevancy becomes a mute issue. Teach an individual what is the very best of his or her human existence, and there will be no need to prove or market what has become apparent through the process of self-acceptance. The need to use frivolous and unreliable props such as class, gender, race, ethnicity, or religion will no longer be thought to be necessary. Also thought to be unnecessary will be the desire to support inequities and inequalities when self-doubt steals its way into the thought process.

The lack of fairness or justice often comes into play in order to fall back on a distorted sense of legitimacy when using the soul killer of comparison. Victims automatically reach for this weapon when measuring one's self to another person or group. Self-discovery and self-acceptance regarding inherent value removes any call to employ the weapon of comparison, which only serves to perpetuate a personal sense of inferiority. Moreover, train a person to prove personal worth to achieve relevance and credibility, and he or she learns through life experiences one definitive result. When a person elevates another individual or group to a position of power to decide the issue of legitimacy, efforts to persuade the source of his or her relevance and worth will simply never be enough. The treadmill representing accommodation remains in perpetual motion in the futile attempt to satisfy unreasonable demands and expectations.

So long as external and material rankings determine importance or unimportance, relevance or its lack, another definitive conclusion is reached. The opportunity to discover the merits of character that determine personal authenticity and value remain vague perceptions. Unless there is a willingness to explore his or her inherent value, such abstractions will remain as such, and out of reach for the person truly in search of genuine personal meaning and purpose. Also out of reach will be the ability to protect one's self from the chaos and fatal attraction to the seductive power of that person or persons who reject a core principle of personal development. Rebuffed is the idea that genuine personal value and moral distinction is relative to good character. Such a way of life is thought to assume a posture of vulnerability and weakness; therefore, unintelligent.

To maintain a safe distance from a lack of accountability, transparency, vulnerability, and blame that favors the pursuit for relevance through deception and dominance is extremely difficult. It is difficult to sidestep mean-spirited and misleading intentions when what is being stated appears quite polished and genuine, but lacks sincerity. By mistaking respect for credibility, it is also difficult to know when a person is seeking from others what he or she refuses to give to others. Every person is in pursuit of relevance and credibility, but not every person is willing to extend him or herself to recognize the two points of personal value in others. In a very sad fashion, generation after generation of human souls have come and gone, only to pass one another as mere ships passing at night. This way of life due in large part is due to a nonexistent or restricted education to the development of character.

To avoid the mirage that promises to be the watering hole where personal thirst for credibility and relevance are fulfilled requires an education with a focus on the inherent gifts of character. Identification, acceptance, and value regarding the innate gifts are the explicit focus that help the individual to distinguish between credibility and relevance contingent upon proof from that not subject to any conditions. With this education, an individual learns that he or she is not defined by experiences, but by the merits of character. Without this education, conditions of compliance that coexist with every tantalizing mirage go unnoticed and certainly lacks any importance when in the tangled web of the oasis.

The inclination to endure the hardship brought on by the contempt that accompanies the notion that something is better than nothing can break the heart. In contrast, when the education to the inherent gifts of character have become an indispensable guide for his or her daily life, the seductive illusion or mirage are viewed as ineffective. Such an education is also paramount in learning how to distinguish between complication and complexity, respect and credibility, and doing that which is right versus good. The high-hanging fruit made available to him or her willing to climb the ladder of introspective thought is an achievement made accessible by discovering the innate gifts of good character.

With that in mind, humanity continues to invite one specific disparaging narrative into its history books. Despite the ever-presence of religion or enlightened thought with respect to climate, energy, medicine, and technology, this narrative remains the same. The fact that very little thought and action has been taken to educate and teach a more realistic blueprint for determining and evaluating relevance remains a disgrace. On the other hand, it is quite understandable as to why this initiative has never been taken seriously, nor acted upon. Far too many people who have attained credibility primarily through external and material means to bolster *what* he or she is would face the challenge to discover qualifications that are more substantial. Advantages once made available to divulge a person as pertinent or prominent evaporate.

Inequalities and inequities arising from class, religious, gender, race, ethnic, and educational differences would decline in favor of achieving a more genuine form of relevance and credibility. Just days prior to his assassination, Jesus, the central figure for Christianity and leader of an egalitarian social reform, is said to have argued for an authentic form of credibility and relevance. His idea of a bona fide legitimacy and significance had to do with the qualities of good that comprise *who* a person is inherently. Standing between the Roman elite, Jewish bureaucrats and religious leaders on one side, and his fellow countrymen and women on the other side, Jesus dared to voice a piercing statement to all that gathered. He brought forth a proclamation that humanity continues to defiantly resist and distract from even to this date in time.[5]

---

[5] *Holy Bible (Authorized King James Version) Luke*: Chapter 17:20–21, "And when he [Jesus] was demanded of the Pharisees, when the kingdom of God should come, he answered them and said, the kingdom of God cometh not with observation: Neither shall they say, lo here! or, lo there! for, behold, the kingdom of God is within you."

Based on the nature of the information and surrounding living conditions, several assumptions can be made as to the narrator's intentions, conversation, and calculated results, From the start, it appears that Jesus calls upon his fellow countrymen and women to stop expressing discontent and sorrow for the overall social deterioration, political corruption, failing crops, rising taxes, and demand for more tithes. Just as importantly, for the declaration to be effective, Jesus urged the people to stop defining themselves, individually and collectively, solely by their experiences. The forthcoming statement would eliminate any further need to create a self-perception aided by the analogy their glass was half-empty, and the glasses of the Roman elite, Jewish bureaucrats, and religious leaders were half-full.

As a point of emphasis, any identification with half-empty or half-full concepts that relate to economic and social circumstances can be counterproductive. Efforts to advance the glass to half-full from empty or full from half-full will necessarily require measures of exploitation, deception, and corruption. Because the glass analogy is a reference made to external economic and social conditions, inequalities and inequities are created in order to attempt the advancement. The evolution of moral and character development remains detached from the analogy and reference to the glass half-empty or half-full.

Jesus apparently knew this, as well as knowing how the intense feelings of longing and yearning for external recognition of credibility and relevance can also be a great source of human pain and suffering. Pleading for accountability, compassion, and change from indifferent external sources vested in fulfilling their self-interest is an absolute waste of time. Instead, Jesus encouraged his fellow countrymen and women to take personal responsibility to change their living conditions, as much as possible. The people had to be reminded of this intervening measure with one penetrating declaration that would declare how the Roman elite, Jewish bureaucrats, and religious leaders were not in total charge of defining their lives.

By taking personal responsibility, the issues of credibility and relevance were, in fact, in their hands. Jesus urged the people to go within and proclaim the "Kingdom of God (good) within you": within each man, woman, and child. Through the discovery of the innate value pertaining to his or her qualities of good character lies the hidden talents that help reveal solutions to address the issues for living life versus surviving. Each man, woman, and child is afforded the opportunity to establish credibility and relevance based on the personal empowerment developed through his or her qualities of good character.

The above mentioned narrative reportedly given by Jesus is referenced for one definitive reason, rather than narratives taken from Abraham, Moses, the Prophet Muhammad, Mahatma Gandhi, Rosa Parks, Nelson Mandela, Martin Luther King Jr., Desmond Tutu, Susan B. Anthony, the 14th Dalai Lama, Benazir Bhutto, or Helen Keller. In their unique and gallant manner, these, and many other courageous individuals not cited here, fought for the same as did Jesus: the issues of credibility and relevance. However, Jesus stands apart from this group of heroes and heroines because his main focus was on establishing legitimacy and relevance based on *who* a person is inherently.

The courageous men and women from the pages of history fighting for the issues of credibility and relevance fought the good fight. Nonetheless, the primary focus propelling the struggles had more to do with *what* an individual is in terms of external circumstances, such as economic and social injustices. For example, the lack of credibility due to being a Jew, Muslim, Indian, woman, South African, and African American were the central issues. This is not to take anything away from the altruistic endeavors and sacrifices made to improve the human condition and life, because the ground gained in advancing humankind beyond entrenched boundaries of bigotry and discrimination did indeed occur.

The problem with the advances made have been the inability to sustain such progress and gains without the tendency to repeat old pain and suffering around human differences, such as class, race, ethnicity, religion, and gender. As a footnote to the narrative, there is no need to be concerned whether Jesus actually spoke the words. What is of great importance is the statement itself. Whether the statement was a product of the era in which it was written, originated from the writer, or Jesus, is of little to no concern. The fact remains apparent; the words were spoken. And when truth comes to life, it is felt immediately, and without pause. This is a great example of that moment in time when truth spoke to power and the powerless. *Who* an individual is with respect to the merits of his or her character will go a long way to improving the chance for success with day-to-day challenges.

The ability to bring to his or her life sound character allows a person to define him or herself by more than the daily encounter of good and less-than-good experiences. During his or her day, a person may confront class intolerance, racial prejudice or discrimination, gender bias, or religious superiority. At the same time that either of these experiences are taking place, on a more profound level below the nonsensical, another experience is materializing. The knowledge that he or she is not irrelevant or inferior to another individual or group, nor the attempt to suggest otherwise takes over the experience. Such a personal recognition moves an individual beyond persevering to developing the qualities of character defined as perseverance and patience. Learning to live versus simply surviving comes about through the evolution of good character.

Nevertheless, this process will remain a mere abstraction if an individual is unable to personally learn how to measure credibility and relevance by a useful standard. The most profound means to accurately measure personal legitimacy and significance come from within the person. When personally accepted, the countless inherent good qualities that each person embodies unite an individual to him or herself, as well as that which morally binds one human being to another. To lack this personal development is to also fall short of understanding how what is considered right is not always good, but what is good will always be right. Subjugation, discrimination, or bias in favor of or against a person or group based on class, race, ethnicity, age, gender, or religion may be considered the right move to make in preserving the status quo, but not a good deed to practice. When the education to developing the merits representing good character is absent from personal growth, the need to be right is greater than the need to be good and to do good.

Sound character evolves into sustainable credibility, and establishes genuine relevance. However, when authority is equated with power and thus, relevance, the vital distinction between what is a right endeavor to take on versus what is a good endeavor to undertake becomes complicated and twisted. A failure to take into account the well-being of others when advancing an idea or act that represents a personal belief or value thought to be the right activity to pursue is motivated by one notion: self-indulgence. The move to advance an idea or act of good that includes and enhances the well-being of others, irrespective of background, represents the difference between character and self-interest. It is important to remember, the act of good is a tide that lifts all boats, while that which is right is a wave that lifts the boats of a limited few.

Again, when the act is considered the right endeavor to pursue but lacks an element of good that reaches beyond the originator's doorstep, then what is considered right is not good. To sell this idea to an audience outside the originator's control, deception comes into play. The conversation is designed to deceive by stating what he or she does not mean, and what is actually meant is withheld for purposes of disguising self-interest and self-indulgence. Adding to the manipulation will be a statement suggesting the act or deed is right and therefore, good. It is easy to mistake complexity for complication when character development is lacking.

The execution of what is considered right driven by self-interest and self-indulgence simply complicates any attempt to justify that it is good. Whereas, the practice and execution of an act of good drills down layer to layer, revealing the legitimacy of both the provider and recipient. To establish credibility and relevance on both sides of a relationship requires good and sound character having been recognized on at least one side. Complexity can never be confused with complication, since it is about discovering depth, while complication is about covering up and concealing depth.

Even when the pursuit of personal relevance and credibility is at the expense of another person or group, violence, discrimination, and prejudice are still considered rational and justified. A way of life fixated on recognizing the lone value of a person as relevant based on *what* he or she is externally and possesses materially guarantees the widespread existence of evil and injustice. The lack of well-intentioned resources willing to educate an individual to value and practice substantive character is the main reasons why such practices dominate the human landscape. Educate a person to know what is the worthiest aspect of his or her human existence and the personal recognition of sustainable legitimacy and relevance become imminent. The good qualities of character will always be an individual's worthiest human component. Derived from the inherent gifts of good character, the new rational and justifiable is the emergence of a reliable and noncompetitive relevance that seeks to make a reality of coexistence.

Violence, contempt, discrimination, and prejudice are nothing more than tactics used to protect a distorted and often perverted self-perception of relevance and superiority. No matter the harm inflicted upon another person or group, the end justifies the means. Again, even if the pursuit of relevance and distinction are at the personal erosion of another person or person's dignity, this is considered reasonable when a way of life is based on finite resources. *What* a person is externally and what he or she possesses materially limits the number of credible persons at the table of prominence. As distorted and often perverted this thinking is, it is crucial to understand that the driving force is to satisfy a basic human instinct of relevance.

Also vital to understand is how futile and self-defeating it is to challenge the cruel and insensitive use of absolute power with power. Oftentimes when an individual is impacted in a harmful way by abusive behavior, the immediate reaction is to exert the identical or similar abusive behavior as a means of retaliation. However, the lack of integrity has never, nor will it ever, stop, bring to justice, or heal the internal and external injuries that result from the lack of integrity. Only the victim who has internalized the mentality of victimization will seek to retaliate in kind against the abusive use of privilege and entitlement with the abusive use of power.[6]

When distinction and authority are determined by external and material achievements, relevance is often attained with the help of distortion and corruption. To conceal the practice of deception due to the limited seating at the table of prominence are the inequities and inequalities. Such human-made imbalances are prevalent and every attempt is made to wrap the unfair practices in a veil of vagueness and duplicity. But, as long as accommodation is the foundation by which relationships are formed within this way of life driven by external gratification, it becomes obvious the associations are mostly synthetic.

It does not matter what class, gender, race, ethnicity, religion or not, credential or not; the link that unites relationships can be

---

[6] *The True Holy War, The Clash Between What We Are Externally vs. Who We Are Intrinsically*; essay on What You Are vs. Who You Are, pages 70–73; Lorenzo D. Leonard; Strategic Book Publishing, New York, New York, Copyright 2009.

described as a drug-affected alliance. Accommodation is the drug that has individuals, verbally and nonverbally, promise to provide for one another's credibility and relevance through a multitude of traditions, customs, and rituals. *Who* an individual is in terms of character traits, such as transparency, vulnerability, accountability, generosity, and being a good person do not matter. Such qualities are not located at the top of the priority list, but much further down after the prerequisites for accommodation have been identified.

Preconditions such as the right physical makeup, lifestyle, class, race, ethnicity, religion or not, career or job, social achievements, and in many instances, political affiliation, are at the top of the list. However, the most vital precondition inclusive of all the above named is the willingness to run the gauntlet of providing protection against having to experience personal insecurities. Not having to look internally and examine his or her personal portfolio to discover inherent gifts that resolve the issues of credibility and relevance are the reasons for using the drug, accommodation. The fact remains, very few individuals are willing to let go of his or her relevance provided by a way of life that equates legitimacy with *what* a person is externally and possesses materially.

The notion that something is better than nothing holds true . . . until the time arrives when that something is worse than nothing. Relationships, and to a great extent, marriages and romantic unions are initiated on this basis: something is better than nothing. Generally speaking, many partnerships are formed for the intended purpose of attaining legitimacy and relevance. Examples would include matrimony, children, extended family, career, the luxurious home/condo, and lifestyle, which include access to sex, money, fashion, recreational drugs, drinking, and gambling.

In regards to the question of whether to pursue a romantic relationship, it is always prudent to follow the four levels of intimacy to ensure cross-examination is adequately answered. In this way, he or she will avoid choosing an inappropriate partner and sidestep a need to use the drug of accommodation. With a way of life principally based on *who* a person is intrinsically, the four levels of intimacy allow him or her to explore the depths of character prior to making a decision whether a romantic and sexual involvement is necessary.

Following the steps of intimacy also allows a person to safeguard against being internally seduced by a need for companionship or to be loved for the purpose of feeling relevant and credible. Adhering to the four levels also helps to safeguard against external presentations disguised to look like genuine interest, but instead, are based on self-interest and utilitarian value.[7] Integrity can protect against experiencing, at a future date, the unfavorable consequences of making a decision to enter into a romantic relationship mostly on the *what*, or external appeal.

The prerequisite for any successful relationship, be it friendship, romantic, or marriage, is the demonstration of meritorious character, especially at the beginning of the association. Perhaps more often than not, differences in all shapes and form will take place. So long as the qualities of admirable character are present to ensure a favorable journey, a beneficial conclusion will be forthcoming. And this result can be said for any relationship. Accountability, transparency, vulnerability, compassion, mutual consideration, and personal responsibility guarantees not necessarily what an individual may desire, but what he or she needs.

However, if an obsession with immediate gratification outweighs prudence, rough times to come are almost a certainty. Seeking meaning and purpose outside of one's self can have disappointing results. The need to have companionship, to be loved, relevant, and credible cannot be the mirage. Nor can the need be fixated upon an

---

[7] *The True Holy War, The Clash Between What We Are Externally vs. Who We Are Intrinsically*; essay on What You Are vs. Who You Are, pages 54–57; Lorenzo D. Leonard; Strategic Book Publishing, New York, New York, Copyright 2009.

intended object. If this persists, the internal scolding is unleashed that is trained to define one's self by experiences. The consequence is to strengthen the notion his or her glass is half-empty or even empty. Either choice will depend on how deeply held the obsession.

Level one represents the ability to share physical space and time void of any inclination to acquiesce or inflate, and with autonomy and equality well-defined. If both persons pronounce level one satisfactory, individually and collectively, the choice to move to level two can be made with mutual consent. Level two allows for the opportunity to share respective ideas or concepts about life, work, politics, religion, and general beliefs. Again, the absence of an inclination to acquiesce or inflate for the purpose of impressing the other, and with autonomy and equality well defined hopefully are present. Both individuals have a basic feeling of good about the other and self, and both feel mutually pleased with the experience. Based on the experiences of level one and the information shared on level two, a sound decision can be made of whether level three is a desirable choice.

If level three is a mutually agreed upon stage to move forward with, both individuals enter a phase in the relationship where accountability, transparency, and vulnerability are reciprocal and expected. If the relationship is to continue with autonomy and equality well defined, it is important that such qualities of character be out in the open for each to experience. This level of intimacy is where individuals learn a great deal about the character and internal makeup of one another, as well as one's self. The sharing of feelings and emotions related to past and current experiences, both good and otherwise, help to determine how an individual handles the issues of conflict and success. This is where a person will learn whether personal resentments are still alive or dead, learn about the existence of any prejudice and bias toward other individuals and/or groups of people.

Level three will reveal whether the drug of accommodation is expected to play a role in the relationship. Without question, this level of disclosure will unveil how each individual personally defines him or herself. It will be either by life experiences, which produce a victim mentality, or by the merits of his or her characters. Also, this is where the separation between polite respect and genuine credibility takes place for each individual. If this separation cannot occur, it is doubtful any meaningful relationship can last or even exist. Polite respect gives off a pretense of being interested in a person. A person knows that he or she is being responded to as possessing genuine credibility, because the individual standing opposite is engaged with his or her individuality.

By the time level three has been successfully experienced, a mutually agreed upon decision can be reached whether level four is a necessary stage to enter: sexual involvement. Relationships that take on long-term intention due to the expectation of a romantic involvement are encouraged to follow levels one through three to determine the appropriateness of sexual involvement. Marriage is usually a concluding result of a long-term romantic relationship with sexual involvement consummating the vows.

It is important to remember that a marriage based on *who* we are intrinsically is more apt to be mutually successful with sexual involvement celebrating the union, rather than being a bounty. Establishing a friendship instead of marriage and without the sexual content can simply be all that the relationship can fathom to support both individuals. The three levels of intimacy will certainly reveal this information. The premature introduction of sex into a relationship can undermine the effort to keep autonomy, equality, and respect well defined for both individuals.

The less a person understands, appreciates, and accepts his or her intrinsic value, the more driven that individual will be to seek the feeling of relevance and credibility from available external sources. This is why in a way of life based on *what* people are externally sex is equated with love, career and money are equated with security, and physical appeal with prominence. When committed to a way of life that is based on *what* people are externally, level four is normally inverted to level one. The need to have another person or thing mainly responsible for one's own well-being is indeed a common approach with a way of life established on *what* people are externally. This is the role of accommodation; the drug that must keep giving. And to conduct this maneuver through sex and other external means because an internal state of emotional and spiritual impoverishment exists is also a common approach.

The need to satisfy an appetite to be seen, heard, and valued is simply a constant denominator with a way of life principally based on achieving relevance and credibility through external means. Again, there is only room for a few at the table of prominence. Relationships, and especially marriages, have a difficult time being successful in terms of longevity, because the drug of accommodation can only maintain a state of bliss for a limited time period. Conversely, with a way of life based on *who* people are intrinsically, relationships, and especially marriages, experience a high degree of success. Why? Because the awareness of being complete and relevant originate from within the individual. Therefore, relevance and credibility are easily recognized by the person as an inherent value. And the four levels of intimacy will help to accentuate this reality.

Rather than develop an appreciation for the character and individuality of the person, the rules for accommodation will dominate the relationship landscape and minimize intrinsic value. This is true wherever the *what* factor plays a major role in determining personal value. Cooperation and compliance is an absolute necessity when it involves attaining prominence and relevance based on the *what* factor. Love fills the air and is frequently spoken of . . . so long as the drug, accommodation, is maintaining its level of bliss. But, like any high-performing drug, the dosage will need to steadily increase in order to fulfill its pledge to provide credibility and relevance.

Accommodation is never enough unless the dosage is frequently increased: the treadmill has to increase its speed if the synthetic association is to persevere. Falling back on inequalities and inequities also helps to ensure a measure of importance when the level of rapture begins to lessen.

For instance, when struggling to experience credibility and relevance in the workplace or social setting, oftentimes relying on economic, gender, race, ethnic, age, and religious differences can help rediscover relevance. Even though this is based on a false sense of well-being, it still serves the purpose of getting through personal uncertainty. The notion that something is better than nothing, again, holds true . . . until the time arrives when that something commits the act of betrayal. External sources used for the purpose of attaining relevance will often determine accommodation to no longer be a viable option. For example, a radical drop in the relevance of seniors due to age and fixed incomes, children leaving home to begin their life, mandatory retirement, marriage partners having run out of options to accommodate each other's personal insecurities, and the decline in the physical and intellectual appeal due to falling short of external standards.

Once more, drawing upon the earlier analogy reportedly stated by Jesus when questioned by the church leaders as to when the Kingdom of God (good) should appear, he said, "The Kingdom of God (good) cometh not with observation: Neither shall they say, lo here! or, lo there! for, behold, the Kingdom of God (good) is within you." The drug of accommodation is never needed nor are external sources in the form of traditions, customs, rituals, or another individual needed to establish personal credibility and relevance. The inherent qualities of good character are more than enough to satisfy the basic human instinct to feel credible and relevant. The idea that a social contract exists between human beings is not imaginary.

By the very nature of the similarities, this is difficult to deny. It is quite real, and it is an indispensable component for personal development, which once recognized and made reality, is insulated by a moral dignity. The lesson is well learned when an individual seeks to be the best that he or she can be and along this path be in a position to support and assist others to be the best that they can be in terms of relevance and credibility. The development of strong moral qualities, such as empathy, integrity, courage, fortitude, honesty, loyalty, generosity, and community will always include other people. The reason being is because the social contract represents the highest degree of partnership the human species can create among one another: a gathering of equals.

The following statement is often made with respect to the text contained within this chapter: "All of this information regarding the steps to genuine intimacy and the pathway to meaningful credibility and relevance are simply way too much for any person to attempt. It takes the fun out of just living life and establishing relationships. A person might as well go and become a monk and live in isolation." There is no question as to the demand asked of any person who desires credibility and relevance that does not come and go due to conditions set forth by the uncertainty of external sources. Much is required of any person interested in his or her romantic relationship or marriage having more than a 50 percent chance of success, which includes longevity, veritable love, mutuality, and room to grow, both individually, as well as collectively.

In order to achieve any of the just mentioned goals, learning to recognize, appreciate, and develop the inherent gifts of his or her character will actualize such tall objectives. Sure, this new way of life is a challenge to achieve, especially within a system of living obsessed with attaching value to what is fabricated to look and appear as the genuine article. The pain and suffering from having made decisions not in his or her best interest is reason alone to justify taking the challenging road ahead. Settling for something, because it is better than nothing no longer is an option. A person is better off alone living with credibility and relevance due to his or her gifts of character, rather than living with someone or something that reminds her or him of being irrelevant, not enough, or unworthy.

Chapter Three

TOO MANY CONCESSIONS!

*"Yet taught by time, my heart has learned to glow
for other's good, and melt at other's woe."*

Homer
Ancient Greek Poet—Odyssey and Iliad

There is little mystery as to understanding the primary motivation to pursue relationships within a system of living that predominantly recognizes material and external value as a keystone to evaluating personal usefulness. In support and in step with this way of life is a philosophy, "the end justifies the means." With this system, there is a race to achieve credibility and relevance based on material and external value. It stands to reason that with this way of life every man is out for himself, and every woman is out for herself. A process, "the means justify the end," is of no use for a material and external-based value system. For purposes of achieving credibility and relevance, relationships formed within this system of living are further motivated by need, rather than by a process that justly satisfies a want. Deficient in the foundation of an education to understand the value and development of character, where genuine credibility and relevance are learned, a different learning experience transpires.

To offset this insufficiency, credibility and relevance are taught to originate outside an individual. However, to pursue this specific track will be at a substantial cost to the ability to live one's life based on his or her personal choices reflective of individuality, authority, and autonomy. Far too many personal concessions will be made in order to attain credibility and relevance from external sources. One cost to the individual is the gradual erosion of the prospect to develop independence and self-government. For example, what religion to serve, what God to worship, what political party to affiliate with, where to live, how to dress, who to play with, socialize with, to date, and to marry are just a few of the concessions made to appease to avoid being deprived of conditional acceptance.

Instead of being taught to develop and rely on the inherent traits of good character to define credibility and relevance, establishing a dependence on external assessments for such achievements are the preferred method for personal development. Establishing a reliance upon external sources for credibility and relevance are deficient in sustainability. In addition, the less an individual is independent of cultural and societal controls, the more he or she can be controlled. Class, race, ethnicity, religion, politics, and gender will seek the concession of individuality in exchange for identification.

Because personal value is linked to the acceptability by external and material sources, and the need to feel relevant is crucial to a person's well-being, concessions of major implications are made to dispassionate sources to attain and maintain that end goal. Other concessions that are made with major personal implications include substituting yes for no and no for yes; vindictive for forgiveness; power for strength; immediate gratification for perseverance and patience; self-indulgence for integrity; the weapon of comparison for commonality; discrimination and prejudice for equality; evil for good; blame for accountability; vague and dubious for transparency; vanity for humility; mean-spirit for generosity; apathy for compassion; stubborn for responsive; bullying for mutuality; ritual and doctrine for practice; and deception for truth.

Concessions made to please an external source to assure some level of credibility simply exemplifies an act of self-betrayal. The act becomes even more problematic when concessions that substitute accommodation, performance, and bliss for love; going along to get along for individuality; aggression for assertiveness; religion, religious superiority, and wars for God; complicity and compliance for freedom; and control and domination is resorted to in place of community. Personal identity attached to any grouping or groupings such as class, race, ethnicity, gender, religion, age, and political affiliations offer limited credibility and relevance in exchange for concessions that weaken personal authority, distinction, and self-determination.

Educate a man, woman, or child to his or her best elements of the human existence, which are the merits of good character, and concessions that undermine credibility and relevance are nonexistent. Concessions cannot be mistaken to have the same purpose as compromise. To concede is to grant or surrender in response to a demand or expectation, whereas, compromise represents an agreement or settlement acceptable to all parties concerned. What is lost or never thought of during the process of surrendering personal empowerment is how conditional credibility and relevance attained in the exchange is never quite as satisfying for the individual in the long-term as it was in the short-term. Over the long haul, failure to erase or drown out the realization and the accompanying pain of participating in acts of self-betrayal for what amounted to meaningless accolades and congratulations can be torturous. Falling for the seduction of the mirage thought to be an oasis can hurt quite deeply with the realization of self-abandonment.

Where there is little to no sense of one's personal value outside the material and external realm, a person becomes easy prey for a way of life promising credibility and relevance at a nominal price. Nothing is free or without consequences, not even distorted credibility and relevance. Addictions that develop from alcohol, drugs, sex, food obsession, starvation, gambling, work, compulsive spending, crime, violence, and the preoccupation with making money are symptoms of a greater ill.

The lack of personal value and the inability to define one's self other than through experiences strengthens an impotency with respect to feeling credible and relevant. The short-term gain of being able to distract from his or her pain through the addiction renders the individual accepting of distorted realities through the fleeting periods of euphoria. Even distorted credibility and relevance are short-lived. Conceding personal dignity to an external source that offers nothing but self-contempt in return results in a person remaining unaware of his or her true value.

The education that teaches an individual to recognize, develop, and value the attributes of good character will also be the source of intelligence that establishes a framework for moral stability. Individuality and self-determination will be protected from the nagging intrusion of impoverishment revealed through self-indulgence. In addition, the ability to grasp exactly what the difference is between short- and long-term gains will provide more success in terms of good choices, rather than accumulating mounds of regret. Impatience and immediate gratification will bear less satisfaction in comparison to patience with the process, which ensures success one way or another. Such realizations are mostly lacking in the thought process when the education of substantive character is deficient.

However, accumulating mounds of regret due to the influence of immediate gratification can force a moment or two of introspective thought to seek a solution for the unwanted problem. The rush to fulfill a want or need can be an attempt to compensate for not having a sense of one's true value, whereas sprinting into credibility and relevance with immediate gratification fueling the dash will quickly resolve the insecurity. That great job, title, position, income, sex, marriage, parenthood, home, automobile eventually can become a heavy burden to morally carry. This is especially true when the personal cost for such achievements was conceding the credibility and relevance of his or her merits of character, which define inherent worth as a person.

Often overlooked are the consequences when a negative is used in the attempt to prove a positive. The first consequence with any certainty will pertain to the net result proving a negative. In contrast, a positive will consistently prove out a positive as a net result. As basic and fundamental as this truth is, humanity continues to struggle with and clash unsuccessfully against its principled soundness. The global community remains absent from the table of progressive thinking when it comes to committing to an appropriate course of action to achieve personal relevancy and importance.

Develop an educational system that teaches the value and practice of good character, rather than continuing to use a system of living that supports a negative approach to achieving credibility. Deficient in sociable instincts and practices, exploitation, corruption, and distortion in collaboration with the act of concession play major roles in attaining relevance. Conceding the best human elements available to achieve personal credibility, which are the attributes of good character, for the negative takes precedence.

In an attempt to prove a positive, self-importance and self-indulgence easily exemplify the negative when one's personal value is attached to class, religion, race, ethnicity, gender, prominence, political affiliation, and physical prowess. The endeavor to prove a positive through means that undermine civility and integrity can only produce a negative result, no matter how appealing the gain. Because there is an absence of qualities such as accountability, transparency, mutuality, and personal responsibility, a vacuum is created instead of the traits that depict ethical credibility.

To help make the transition into this artificial form of credibility as opaque as possible, satisfaction with the result is verbally expressed with great joy in order to distract people from realizing the misguided rationale—*the end justifies the means*—was used to achieve the desired goal. The global financial crisis of 2007–2008 was principally overshadowed in the United States by homeowners taking on bad mortgages to ill-advisedly pursue the American dream. This and an underqualified workforce unemployed were publicized as major contributors for the collapse. This reporting pitted Americans against Americans, rather than focusing the primary contributor for the financial crisis in the United States on the greed of banks, insurance companies, and financial managers.[8]

The banking and financial industries took full advantage of an unqualified buying public to gain records profits that included betting between one another the risky mortgages would fail, which were labelled derivatives and credit default swaps. The U.S. Senate's Levin-Coburn Report reported that the crisis was the result of "high risk, complex financial products; undisclosed conflicts of interest; the failure of regulators, the credit rating agencies, and the market itself to rein in the excesses of Wall Street."

The Financial Crisis Inquiry Commission concluded that the financial crisis was avoidable and caused by widespread failures in financial regulation and supervision, dramatic failures of corporate governance and risk management at many systemically important financial institutions, a combination of excessive borrowing, risky investments, and lack of transparency by financial institutions, ill preparation and inconsistent action by government that added to the uncertainty and panic, a systemic breakdown in accountability

---

[8] *Senate Financial Crisis Report*, 2011 (PDF). Retrieved April 22, 2011.

and ethics, collapsing mortgage-lending standards and the mort-gage securitization pipeline, deregulation of over-the-counter de-rivatives, especially credit default swaps, and the failures of credit rating agencies to correctly price risk.[9]

Adding insult to injury, President Barack Obama appointed Tim Geithner, former head of the New York Federal Reserve, and Larry Summers, former treasury secretary under President Bill Clinton, to head-up the Treasury and the White House National Economic Council respectively, at the start of his first term. Both appoint-ments to key economic positions were criticized on grounds that both Geithner and Summers had been prominently involved in creating many of the conditions that led to the financial crisis of 2007–2008; so failure is being rewarded. Summers was a leading advocate of the derivatives deregulation, together with Alan Greenspan and Robert Rubin. And during his transition to Secretary of the Treasury, the act that kept commercial banks out of Wall Street, the Glass-Steagall Act, was repealed. Geithner instead was criticized for his failure to pay $34,000 in income taxes.[10]

The underlying cause for social injustice, religious and secular wars, economic and financial calamities are linked to the ill-advised thinking—*the end justifies the means*—being injected at the beginning of the misfortune. However, to welcome this style of thinking and its subsequent accomplishments lays the basis to accept a counter-productive measure opposed to establishing relationships based on

---

[9] Final Report of the National Commissions on the Causes of the Financial and Economic Crisis in the United States: Official Government Edition: *The Financial Crisis Inquiry Commission*: Submitted by Pursuant to Public Law 111–21, January 2011.

[10] Final Report of the National Commissions on the Causes of the Financial and Economic Crisis in the United States: Official Government Edition: *The Financial Crisis Inquiry Commission*: Submitted by Pursuant to Public Law 111–21, January 2011. Timothy Canova (25 November 2008), "*Obamanomics: Is this real change?*" The Real News. Retrieved December 13, 2008.

equality. This particular logic is based on self-indulgent reasoning, which easily becomes addictive when associated with privilege and entitlement. Any person or group committed to this rationale simply will not recognize the legitimacy of any class, race, ethnicity, religion, and gender outside of its realm of familiarity.

What's more, when *the end justifies the means* is used to achieve a goal, ethical standards will not be preferred methods used to reach a desired objective. In its place will be the misuse and abuse of authority to make certain the goal is realized. *The end justifies the means* is motivated by an attitude that reveals the only sacredness of human life with any presumed meaning pertains to the person or group employing this rationale. Credibility and relevance are restricted to the person or group leading the charge to accomplish the end result by any means possible. And this mandate can include eliminating any person or group from its pathway deemed an obstruction. Appreciation for the sacredness of human life outside of the realm of familiarity is nonexistent. History, be it American, British, Russian, Asian, Eastern European, South American, or Middle Eastern, all are full of examples where the sanctity of human life meant absolute nothing, except to those committed to *the end justifies the means*. This type of manipulation with respect to morality has been a persistent footnote throughout humanity's history.

Humankind is all too familiar with the many faces evil can present, which can transform itself into a highly perverted, distorted, and, of course, quite a cruel adversary. However, the one presentation evil can posture that humanity does not know all that well is the face of subtlety. So delicate, polite, and crafty is the deceptive appearance, yet, armed to discredit and destroy personal value while remaining extremely difficult to detect. Again, concessions are what is being pursued. The promise in exchange is a form of credibility, relevance, and value that a person can develop an identity around without remorse. However, when the *end justifies the means* enters the equation, the face of subtlety also is covertly factored into the equation. Hence, the imminent arrival of a more defined version of evil.

During early American history, for their promise to stop fighting and transition into a docile people, the Native American was promised sovereignty and land to hunt and live on by the United States government. Treaties signed by both parties authenticated the concession and takeover of territories previously occupied by the Native Americans. All such treaties were eventually broken by the U.S. government, and the Native Americans were subsequently moved to barren and isolated reservations. This act of betrayal was further intensified with the intrusion of the subtlety of evil. The undisguised evil of broken treaties and confiscated land was linked to a disguised evil with one cunning maneuver. Small groups of Native Americans were given token privileges and status to help track, capture, and bring to justice rebellious Native Americans refusing to accept initial treaty conditions or new conditions from broken treaties.

Often engaged in armed struggles as a means of protest and retaliation, Native Americans were either killed or captured from such efforts. Captives were routinely handed over to local or government authorities, only to be subjected to extreme harsh conditions. With the aid of Native Americans, who were excellent trackers of their own people, "a house divided eventually collapses." This house divided was quite evident before the white population began their expansion into the territories occupied by the Native Americans. It was not uncommon for Native American tribes to attack one another for food, horses, guns, and to capture other tribesmen and women. This subtlety or covert act of evil initiated from within the group, where the intention is to discredit or destroy another Native American has been a major part of humanity's overall history.

Oppression is often perpetuated by the oppressed who betray its own kind by accepting a conditional credibility and relevance initially set in motion by the original oppressor. The African American was never invited to take an active part in the discussions between the abolitionists, Republican Party, and government officials with respect to freedom versus slavery, but, to the African Americans' surprise, they awoke one morning on January 1, 1863, to learn how the Proclamation and executive order issued in 1862 by President Abraham Lincoln had become effective that day. The Proclamation and executive order declared "that all persons held as slaves are, and henceforward shall be free." The census report of 1860 disclosed there were 3,953,761 slaves, which represented 12.6 percent of the total American (31,443,321) population.[11]

Having been under political pressure since entering office, President Lincoln issued the Emancipation Proclamation for humanitarian reasons, but also to help bring an end to the Civil War by weakening the economic position of the South. The African American would eventually learn the Emancipation Proclamation was issued partly as a political and economic tool, and partly for moral reasons. The utilitarian purpose behind the executive order would explain, in part, a reason for the evil of slavery coming to a close. Yet, right on its heels was another form of evil gaining momentum for which no quick and easy solution would be available: racial prejudice and discrimination.

When the African American walked off the plantation fields of slavery as a free man, woman, and child, all three would step into an American culture, generally speaking, not ready or willing to accept them as legitimate persons. The American culture, during this period, was mostly comprised of European immigrants with a very small percentage of Asian settlers. However, this newly freed newcomer whose genesis began in Africa was not to be counted as an equivalent when it came to defining Americans. The American culture had not been

---

[11] https://en.wikipedia.org/wiki/1860_United_States_Census,The United States Census of 1860 was the eighth Census conducted in the United States starting June 1, 1860 and lasting five months.

emotionally, psychologically, and intellectually prepared to receive the poor, uneducated, and unskilled African American as a credible peer. Though a substantial number of American immigrants were in the identical economic, social, educational, and unskilled position during this time period, one marking made all the difference.

The color of the African American's skin made it easy for other ethnic groups to identify as an ethnic group to discredit, and even destroy if conditions were right. The payoff that accompanied this designation for scorn was to elevate their own credibility and relevance at the expense of the African American. With a cultural résumé filled to capacity as being the ideal target to manipulate for purposes of self-indulgence and self-importance, and having no rights to speak of, the elevation was quite simple. It was not difficult for other ethnic groups to stake a claim of superiority over what was once considered nothing more than chattel. The road to enlightened hearts and minds derived from an education to the value and effectiveness of good character had not taken place, nor would it take place. With a great deal of attention being directed toward building a unified nation and a system of living based on economic and material superiority, concerns with character development were out of the question.

Yes, slavery was a huge contradiction to America's stated declaration: "We hold these truths to be self-evident, that all men are created equal, that they are endowed by their Creator with certain unalienable Rights, that among these are Life, Liberty and the pursuit of Happiness." Such a straightforward declaration of principle has often been referred to as "one of the best-known sentences in the English language," expressing "the most potent and consequential words in American history." The institution of slavery had to be defeated, just as the South had to be defeated and brought back into a federation of states to protect the intended purpose to create a unified nation.

However, once again, the attempt to legislate morality had failed. To educate and appeal to the hearts and minds of the people the moral credibility of a nation committed to the words, "We hold these truths to be self-evident, that all men are created equal" was never a priority. And why should it be when the history of humankind revealed no such previous precedent? Slavery was ended as America had come to experience it, but the brainchild of its manifestation was to remain an obscure problem. Emotional, intellectual, and spiritual impoverishment with respect to the sacredness of human life was left to remain a perplexing abstraction.

As previously stated, oppression is often perpetuated by the oppressed who betray its own kind by accepting conditional credibility and relevance initially set forth by the original oppressor. This unfortunate reenactment was to plague the African American as it had the Native American. Collectively, the African American has lived with the concept "a house divided eventually collapses" since the beginning days of slavery. During this time period, and throughout much of the global community, agriculture required a large labor force to guarantee timely production and delivery to the European markets. Tobacco, cotton, and sugarcane crops were the agriculture bonanza markets demanded. Black Africans were kidnapped within the interior of Africa by black slave traders and delivered to European slave traders awaiting the windfall labor force at the shores of coastal waters. Delivering black Africans to the assembly lines satisfied a much-needed labor force and offered a viable solution for production issues.

The conspicuous evil of slavery instituted by the white entrepreneur was aided by the backroom evil committed by the profit-minded black African slave traders. Because the African interior was mostly disease infected, European slave traders rarely ventured off the coastal shores in search of Africans. Instead, the African slave traders, usually representing powerful tribes, would pursue other natives using trickery or outright kidnapping methods. At the height of the trade during the middle-eighteenth century, an estimated 80,000

Africans left the shores of Western Africa headed for the Caribbean Islands, Brazil, Spanish America, the United States, and Portugal, where the slave trade actually began. Because conditions on board the slave ships were extremely deplorable, many captured Africans died or committed suicide en route to their destination of captivity.

Regarding the Native American's history of betrayal toward its own kind during the westward expansion of America, the same type of betrayal is disclosed throughout the African American's early history with slavery. This history of betrayal first reveals itself when Africans track and capture other Africans for economic gain and for purposes of credibility and relevance. Because European slave traders mainly refused to go into the dense thicket of bushes and trees to capture natives, this provided the black slave trader an opportunity to prove his relevance by initiating the tracking and capture of the natives.

The act of betrayal, African American against African American, could be traced to the slave plantations and beyond. Where the African American was concerned, the owners and overseers of the plantations would use token privileges and conditional credibility to create resentment and hostility between slaves. To pit the field servant against the house servant or field servant against field servant was quite a common practice. In most cases, men and women were separated on the plantations, thus contributing to the long-standing process to emasculate the African American male.

Oftentimes, the same manipulative methods of offering conditional credibility and token favors were continued by the dominant white culture after slavery ended. Such measures were used to create an environment of distrust and jealousy within the African American community. Favors and conditional credibility and were usually given out to the "good nigger," and any African American displaying contrary behavior was labeled a "troublemaker" or "bad nigger." Another area where division occurred concerned skin pigmentation. The lighter the skin pigmentation, the less apprehension the white culture would direct toward the African American.

However, disdain and jealousy would be the reaction from African Americans with darker skin. For that matter, darker pigmentation would draw apprehension from both the African American and white cultures. Not until the African American can step away from taking an active role in the practice of self-inflicted genocide will there be an opportunity to disengage from institutionalized racism. Not until the African American can bring meaning to the phrase given life by Dr. Martin Luther King Jr., "the content of character," will the need to be linked to acts of brutality and evil initiated either from within the culture or outside dramatically decline.

Of course "black lives matter," but until black lives matter to black lives, there is no way that black lives will matter to white, brown, and Asian lives. In addition, not until black lives matter to black lives will black lives matter to the justice, economic, educational, and religious systems. An American football metaphor seems appropriate at this time. To expect or demand any segment of society to appear at midfield or even go beyond that point to recognize the legitimacy and equality of another person or group is absurd. Such a move is absolutely counterproductive and unrealistic.

This is especially true when that person or group has yet to accept this realization, but maintains the expectation and demand from the thirty- or forty-yard line. Laws are in effect to protect all persons and groups from the outward abusive acts of discrimination by another person or group. But, these same laws cannot force a person or group to recognize in his or her hearts and minds the credibility and equality of another person or group. It is a well proven reality that it is impossible to legislate morality. So too is it impossible to force credibility and relevance upon others through acts of violence, intimidation, and coercion.

Educate to the qualities and value of good character, and chances of winning the hearts and minds of others will increase, due to credibility having a more authentic meaning. With disputes over validity and relevance, each involved side is responsible for arriving at the fifty-yard line or midfield. Whether the dispute concerns economic, social, gender, racial, or religious differences, the issue of credibility and relevance has to be mutually agreed upon before resolution can be achieved. The most important agenda for any person or group involved in a conflict with another, which will supersede the resolution, is to reach that fifty-yard line where accountability, transparency, and community take place. Even if the other side is reluctant to come to the halfway point, stay the course.

Educate to the inherent attributes of good character and the need to pursue credibility based on prominence, dominance, or through the eyes of another will no longer matter. Black lives will always matter so long as the transitions out of a state of internalized racism is kept afloat with an education to meritorious character. This way, the transition is made much easier, because the individual is learning how to define his or her self by more than just experiences. Furthermore, black lives will always matter as this group moves away from being a primary target for external sources seeking to discharge impoverishment. This is made possible because the sacredness of human life will finally matter.

In looking back at early American history, many concessions were made by Native and African Americans. Whether the reasons supporting the concessions were to seek relief from harsh intolerance or to artificially inflate self-importance, the cost of not having a more warranted sense of value continues to have consequences for both cultures. No one can fault either culture for submitting to a way of life absent of any example where the attributes of sound character were upheld to be noble and honorable. The sacredness of human life was just as much an abstract notion then as it is during modern times. For that matter, prior to each culture's respective clashes with well-established external oppressive forces, both were internally structured and entrusted to honor the same way of life. Both cultures lacked teaching moral authority through the development of the attributes of sound character.

Both cultures created their respective rituals, ceremonies, and rites of passage to celebrate a physical existence, but not its moral counterpart. No one can fault either culture for morally surrendering to a way of life based on persecution, brutality, and deception for a small portion of relief. However, reality being what it was, in exchange for yielding dignity, integrity, and community, conditional credibility and relevance were the rewards. Token privileges, worthless rankings, and economic gain were granted for tracking, capturing, selling into slavery, or handing over to American authorities a cultural kin. Betrayal, deception, and comparison that led to jealousy and contempt were not new to the internal interactions of either culture. Long before American officials and European slave traders arrived, power and dominance were a way of life for both cultures.

So it makes perfect sense that after slavery ended and the West was settled minus the Native American, both cultures would emulate and duplicate the only system of living they were familiar with: power, prestige, and dominance. The absence of how to achieve and sustain personal dignity, integrity, and community through character development, before their respective periods of oppression, would continue afterward. Throughout the Native and African American's periods of oppression, there were numerous men and women who exemplified good character through strong attributes of dignity and integrity. However, these exemplary individuals were not enough to influence their respective cultures to typify such moral authority. Both Native and African American cultures would go on to uphold a system of living by which credibility and relevance were reserved for individuals attaining value based on *what* he or she was in terms of external and material credentials. Relationships were influenced by the same as the dominant white culture . . . duplicity, deception, and abuse to ensure positions of power, control, and distinction.

Again, with this as the leading social example, concerning a system of living, no one can fault either culture for committing to a way of life that failed to give equal importance to teaching the traits of good character. Established alongside a preoccupation with external and material achievements would have provided a more balanced way of life in terms of lessening the impact of deception and betrayal. To discover the best qualities any human being can possess during his or her lifetime was simply not a socially driven agenda. Such an absence has been occurring since the beginning of humankind. This was first evidenced when Adam and Eve decided to yield to the devil's influence in the Garden of Eden due to a void concerning the value of the inherent gifts of character.

As the Native and African American cultures were conceding the best qualities a human being can possess to attain nothing more than unsustainable and conditional credibility, a similar pattern of engagement was being acted out elsewhere. So too were the same concessions being made by the dominant white culture within their ranks. Not uncommon was the self-indulgent act to pursue and even demand what was in effect conditional credibility and relevance from one another. Self-interest came into play when at the same time refusing to provide the semblance of credibility and relevance to another. Without the education to substantive character, credibility and relevance derived from the inherent gifts of character become the oddity, while its imitation drenched in conditions becomes the standard.

A system of living that basis external and material prominence exclusively with personal value will need an imitation and lookalike to signal credibility and relevance. Absent an equal recognition for the inherent qualities associated with good character, self-indulgence and self-importance will have a commanding influence on relationships.

Because there is a lack of authenticity, transparency, and account-ability, this system of living is a natural breeding ground for betrayal and distrust. The end game is to attain credibility and relevance by any manipulative means available. With the end game primarily focused on external results, the sacredness of human life is extremely vulnerable to the forces of evil.

Racism in America, or in any sector of the global community, lessens when the concerned parties cease from using good, bad, or indifferent personal experiences to define themselves. When there is a lack of knowledge regarding the ability to define one's self other than through experiences, the vacuum is filled with the inept. Humanity will go along with its own incompetent tactic to use income, educa-tion, race, ethnicity, gender, and religion to create divisions among people established on a superior and inferior basis. The real enemy in need of amending will be a way of life that excludes the most effec-tive method to define one's self: the inherent attributes of honorable character.

With the passage of the Nineteenth Amendment to the United States Constitution in 1920, history was made. It was two years after World War I was declared over on November 11, 1918, fifty-five years after the American Civil War ended in the spring of 1865, and slavery was officially ended in December of the same year. With a firm res-olute and many years of impassioned protests behind them, women were finally leveraged to change the course of a male-dominated chronicled history. No longer could the message to a threatened male citizenry and a few hesitant sisters be denied that the time for a wom-an's intelligence and authority be heard at the ballot box. Prior to this momentous period of time, women had long been declined credibility and relevance when it came to making a legitimate contribution to the electoral process.

Baseless arguments that summarized women as lacking the intel-lectual capacity to grasp the complexity of important political, social, economic, and governmental issues were used to counter suffrage protests. Adding fuel to fire, the argument was made by male counterparts that women were inclined to be too emotional. With this being a dominant state of mind, the possibility of relying on rational thought to resolve important issues of state and government would be difficult. Such gender bias and discredit helped to galvanize male resistance toward women being able to experience credibility and relevance concerning voting privileges. However, these same women were expected to welcome into their lives partnerships of marriage, to bear and raise children, provide the entitled male with sexual gratification, maintain a male-dominant household, and serve as caregivers during male-generated wartime activities.

Preceding 1920, conditional credibility and relevance were all that women could possibly achieve in a world that was dominated by the power and control of men. Women had remained both in subordinate and supporting roles of limited power in comparison to that of their male counterparts. Nevertheless, consistent with Native and African American history of concessions, women in varying numbers and degrees contributed to maintaining the role of a subordinate. For reasons of survival, as well as to share in the spoils of male-dominant power, it was not uncommon to concede attributes derived from the genuine and innate feminine. To sustain a nonthreatening level of acceptable credibility and relevance for the male, a legitimate characteristic to a woman's gender and individuality had to be repressed.

To subdue or even extinguish the genuine feminine was a common practice among women. Much to the disappointment of the global community, repression of genuine, inherent feminine attributes remains widespread during modern times. Assisted by women in certain corners of the globe to either dull or exaggerate the feminine appeal, many religious, economic, and social practices conspire to keep the qualities subordinate. Even with the advancements made by women, the male counterpart remains in a dominant role with respect to political and economic power . . . and just as vital, remains comfortably non-threatened by any legitimate attempt on the woman's part to attain full equality.

Nonetheless, what has markedly changed dating back to the 1970s are the advancements women have made throughout much of the free world. Unable to reach full equality with the male counterpart, women have taken a sizable slab out of the political, economic, and social power grid once controlled by men. Rather than being the designated beneficiary for allocated portions of the spoils that filtered down from male dominance and power, women now claim their own spoils. Initiated through their own efforts to exert dominance and power, it was only a matter of time after the historic moment in 1920 that women would begin to flex their relevance and authority. That said, with commanding workforce numbers, solid upper, middle, and lower management positions throughout virtually every industry, women continue committed to fulfilling a basic instinctual female desire: giving birth, raising children, and keeping alive a structure of family.

Adding to this résumé, women have learned quite well how to externally appear charming with respect to what looks like appealing feminine qualities. Inwardly, many among this sex have also learned how to internalize and act out the distorted masculine. Power, strong-willed, and pride in contrast to strength, compromise, and humility trump the genuine feminine in favor of the distorted masculine. Authentic feminine qualities, such as compassion, mutuality, vulnerability, and transparency lack credibility among many women due to living within a lifestyle that primarily honors power and dominance.

The distorted masculine qualities serve the purpose for attaining relevance and credibility with fear as an underlying basis to motivate people. Also, consistent within a system of living that honors power and dominance, attributes that reflect the feminine are viewed as being weak and shallow. As the strengths of good character are learned, valued, and practiced, genuine feminine attributes replace traits of the distorted masculine, such as self-interest, deception, and evasion.

Balance between genuine feminine and masculine qualities of an individual are a direct outcome of character development. But, within a system of living dominated by external and material pursuits in order to achieve credibility and relevance, interest in attaining internal balance is abandoned for the alleged stability of external power and prominence. Conceding the best attributes a person can possess during his or her lifetime to a system of living dominated by power and control produces two human tragedies. Lost to that person or persons making the concessions are the opportunities to experience his or her credible individuality and personal dignity.

When surrendering such vital elements of a person's humanity, the outcome is predictable. It makes no difference whether the concessions are made by women, Native Americans, and African Americans, as well as other ethnic, religious, and social groups; the aftermath is to take on the same attributes as that of the person, group, or doctrine demanding the concessions. Developing personal characteristics similar to that of the dominant and powerful, such as entitlement, insensitivity, instant gratification, and impatience are not uncommon repercussions.

Self-indulgence and self-importance are easily duplicated when dignity and individuality have vacated the personal premises. And the intended purpose of dominating and controlling another human being is to have that individual renounce the best attributes he or she can possess for the perverted pleasure of experiencing conditional credibility. Survival under absolute rule may indeed be the reason to suppress the best attributes a person can possess during his or her lifetime. However, it is very important to understand that suppressing individuality and dignity for the purpose of surviving harsh conditions that punish, discredit, or even threaten human life simply is a short-term solution. If and when such conditions are no longer in effect, because the value and practice of good and sound character has been learned, it is crucial to allow individuality and dignity to resurface. This undertaking is significant if the oppressed are to avoid moving forward in his or her life without emulating the abuse and misuse of power learned at the hands of the absolute ruler.

There are circumstances where the cruel conditions of absolute rule or abuse will never subside. Governments run by a dictator; class, race, and ethnic prejudice; the disregard and disrespect of the young; and religious partiality can produce harsh conditions of living that can last seemingly forever. The objective of any system predicated on absolute rule is to weaken the credibility and relevance of an individual or group in order to preserve its position of power and dominance. The proactive response to such a system is to learn, value, and practice the merits of good character.

Living within a landscape of oppression, it is best to render unto the rule, but serve the principle of good. This response need not be made public, but never internally halted. Perseverance and patience will certainly have their reward. Governance can appear unjust and one-sided. But, if truth is allowed to breathe, this is never so. With the threat to punish, discredit, or even threaten human life facing a person or group on a consistent basis, such knowledge regarding how to live one's life can offer a peace of mind no absolute ruler or abuser can eliminate.

However, the lack of awareness regarding the credibility and relevance of good character can make the personal decision to concede the use of individuality and to protect dignity quite easy. The choice not to question reasons for the surrender to either one's self or the external command is rarely visited. To do what he or she is told to do or simply follow expectations are directives assembled into a system of living that is absent a focus on initiating credibility through character development. When there is a deficiency regarding the education and training of substantive character, the less challenging road to relevance will be pursued.

The inability to recognize inherent credibility and intrinsic value will necessitate creating an unwise dependence on external credentials. This state of affairs is what gives reason for establishing the philosophy, "the end justifies the means." When the only models available to establish credibility and relevance involve developing skills suitable for dominance, exploitation, and corruption, one learning experience is sure to occur. While navigating through the maze of how to be in one's life, it is quite difficult to cultivate an appreciation for the sanctity of human life.

As long as intrinsic value is deemed to be less important than nationalistic pride; political ideology; religious dogma; economic conceit; physical vanity; cultural, ethnic, and racial superiority: sure to occur is another experience. The sacredness of human life will be left with no other fate than to be diminished in favor of acting out self-importance and self-indulgence at the expense of another person or group. Intrinsic value as it pertains to the inherent gifts of meritorious character elevates the meaning of the sanctity of human life to a conscious level. Upon reaching this personal discovery, it becomes apparent that nothing associated with this earthly existence can offer the type of sustainability provided by the most sacred relationship a person can attain through his or her gifts of character.

Except those individuals linking inherent credibility with character, all other relationships will exist under the covering of conditional credibility. Without the personal discovery of inherent credibility and relevance, the value of a human life will mean absolutely nothing while a state of impoverishment internally dominates. In spite of religious, academic, and social intentions to portray the opposite, the expertise applied to intellectual artistry cannot replace the emotional and spiritual understanding that is a result of a personal acceptance of his or her inherent credibility. The attempt to dismiss intrinsic value as irrelevant and elevate conditional credibility achieved through an external sanctuary suggesting paradise has produced one effect. Such futile attempts have simply made humankind just that thirstier, hungrier, angrier, and wanting.

Chapter Four

A NEGATIVE OR POSITIVE?

There can be no vulnerability without risk; there can be no community without vulnerability; there can be no peace, and ultimately no life, without community.

The whole course of human history may depend on a change of heart in one solitary and even humble individual— for it is in the solitary mind and soul of the individual that the battle between good and evil is waged and ultimately won or lost.

M. Scott Peck

When a negative is used in the attempt to prove a positive, the net result is always a negative. A positive will consistently prove out a positive, and the same is correct with a negative resulting in a negative. As basic as this truth is, humanity continues to struggle with and clash unsuccessfully against its principled soundness. To grasp the underlying reasons for this historic dilemma, a person has to begin by recognizing the apparent absence of any genuine effort on humanity's part to cease from engaging in what is simply an act of futility. The global community remains absent from the table of innovative thinking when it comes to generating new ideas that would help itself to better understand and appreciate the value of human life.

When it comes to developing a more reliable path to attaining credibility and relevancy, progressive thinking has not been part of the process. Instead, the approach to elevating the value of human life has been consumed with forceful and bitter verbal attacks that involve either an increase or decrease in regulations with respect to economic and social laws, free speech, religion, guns, and prisons. Advancing the process with the purpose to elevate the sanctity of human life through teaching methods that recognize the strength and value of good character is out of the question to pursue.

However, the course that has been historically chosen, and lacks any innovative thinking, is one that prohibits the global community from advancing toward a more complete understanding of effectual personal authority and relevancy. This historical course has also prohibited the global community from advancing to an understanding that can easily translate into attaining a personal value that is genuine and sustainable. When *what* a person is externally and possesses materially is successfully balanced and in tune with *who* that person is with respect to his or her merits of character, an uncomplicated and distinct life's work emerges. When this particular course of action is pursued, a more sustainable credibility and relevance replaces an external image based on self-importance and self-indulgence.

The personal need to create an overstated or understated identity that conceals internal insecurities, because traits of authenticity are discounted as lacking social appeal, simply evaporates. Accountability, transparency, vulnerability, and thoughtfulness, which are well-defined attributes of character, create a foundation for consistency and longevity to take root. Outside the sphere of like-mindedness, to maintain a position of economic, religious, and social superiority relative to another individual or group requires manipulative action that involves promoting oneself as being more credible and relevant. Though the process is completely manufactured, relevance and credibility are substantiated through highly developed values and beliefs that represent self-interest. This encourages exploitation of external sources for the purpose of achieving superiority and a type of authority that is not to be challenged.

The most common sources exploited to achieve such an agenda are historically based, such as gender, race, ethnicity, religion, economic status, and education. It is not difficult to grasp how inequities and inequalities built into the external sources play a significant role in attaining credibility and relevance. Because relevance is a genuine instinct essential to the human existence, it is easy to understand how its fulfillment by whatever means necessary, is viewed to be an appropriate and correct initiative to enact. Herein lies humanity's unceasing struggle with and unsuccessful clash with a principled soundness: a negative act, if not corrected, will result in a negative conclusion.

With the education to substantive character lacking, and a legitimate instinct to feel relevant and consequential in demand, the outcome is predictable. It is not surprising to learn how an addiction to power, dominance, consumption, and corruption can become the means to satisfy a personal thirst and hunger to feel credible. In addition, any perceived threat to derail this manufactured credibility and relevance will be subject to harsh backlash and cruel treatment, all under the guise of doing what is a person's right to pursue: fulfillment. A system of living that primarily bases credibility on external and material value will support and spin a negative act into a positive one in order to sustain relevance because "the end justifies the means."

This same system solely based on external and material value will dictate what to think, what to believe, and what to feel to necessitate complete control over an individual or group. The rush to racial, ethnic, religious, political, and nationalistic superiority thoroughly capitalize on this agenda. Is there any serious wonder as to why the homeless are sleeping in doorways, mental illness, crime, alcohol and drug addiction, obesity, and starvation remain blatant images in society's mirror?

Any system of living lacking the committed effort to educate its inhabitants to the value and practice of the merits of character leaves only one pathway to define itself. The only method available to determine his or her value is through experiences, good, bad, or indifferent. To seek personal relevance and credibility through the recognition of inherent value derived from honorable character, which is outside conventional means supported by a way of life based on external and material value, places that individual in a precarious position. He or she becomes a target for withdrawal of conditional relevance and credibility from environmental sources.

When expectations of accommodation and compliance are deemed lacking due to efforts to express individuality and self-determination, conditional relevance is replaced with patronizing respect. The individual who dares to step outside of conventional sources to pursue credibility and relevance, such as orthodox religion and politics, race, ethnicity, and relationships based on mutual and reciprocal values runs the risk of being a faction for exclusion. To live his or her life based on the inherent value derived from good character is the qualifier for exclusion. Within a system of living where the sanctity of human life is derived from external and material value, there is little room, if any, at the table representing community for the innate and intrinsic.

It is worth mentioning that both conditional relevance and patronizing respect are superficial, at best. However, patronizing respect tends to be more acidity and demeaning in its attempt to discredit the person. Expectations based on accommodation and compliance are representative of customs and practices established to support inequality and inequity. It is wise to understand that no amount of time devoted to accommodate and comply in order to feel accepted will change conditional relevance and credibility into the genuine article. This condition is easy to discern when mutual and reciprocal actions are absent from relationships.

Again, race, ethnic, religious, economic, political, and nationalistic efforts to maintain a level of superiority follow this agenda quite closely. A negative can only produce a negative, and in this case, moral impoverishment is a natural spin-off. The absence of substantive character will always equal impoverishment. For those individuals who do choose to pursue a calling that honors his or her intrinsic nature and value of meritorious character, the impact upon the larger segment of his or her environment will be negligible in the beginning. However, as an honorable life is lived out, the impact upon his or her surrounding environment will be sufficient to inspire more good: in spite of being excluded.

It is understandable as to why there is a lack of appeal for a way of life that promotes balance, prosperity, and justice on a comprehensive basis. The stature bestowed to *what* a person is in terms of external relevance and material value translates into power, dominion, and prestige over other individuals designated as less relevant. The change required to elevate the attraction of mutual success and impartial justice would necessitate a focused and well-organized segment of humanity. One of the more important challenges at hand would be to restrain itself from taking advantage of the spoils of inequity and inequality: good or bad. This would include the faction of humanity that is victimized by the practice of injustice and discrimination, which is subsequently used to embrace a posture of irrelevance and marginalization.

Be it cultural or societal, doctrine and tradition passed down that justifies any person living under the dominant control and power of another becomes yesterday's history. A demand for the education concerning the merits, value, and practice of character assuredly is the agenda for the segment of humanity seeking to elevate the sanctity of human life. But, who has the determination, let alone time, to voluntarily renounce a system of living that has outlived its intended purpose to link credibility with power? Just as importantly, who has the perseverance and patience to learn a new system that links relevancy with empowerment? Renouncing the benefits attached to *what* a person is externally and possesses materially for far less social and psychological appeal requires more than just an intellectual declaration. A deeply felt awareness that decidedly settles into the emotional chambers declaring self-betrayal is no longer an option to attain credibility, and relevance transforms the declaration into a way of life.

Moreover, who has the courage and fortitude to bring into question a system of living that divides people and downgrades individuality? At the same time division and degradation are occurring, the one pathway for defining one's self that determines credibility and relevance remains the golden rule. This widely accepted illusion for defining personal credibility, or its lack, has also been successful in convincing people how to live their life, what to think, and what to believe based on restrictive information. The final question: who has the patience to develop individuality and thinking on the basis of personal empowerment, principled gratification, and mutual collaboration initiated from a system of living that educates to legitimate credibility?

It is common knowledge that absolute power, instant gratification, and self-interest have proven in many instances to be unsustainable. In the place of answering the personal call to honor his or her intrinsic nature and value of meritorious character, the inescapable adversaries who make the loss of power and prosperity inevitable are self-importance and self-indulgence. The attempt to remedy nagging feelings of lack and unworthiness is further intensified by the preoccupation to feel credible in an urgent and efficient manner. The all-consuming need to feel relevant and connected can easily lead an individual in the direction of a multitude of false securities. Skilled in the art of seduction, social messages that sell the idea that prominence, physical beauty, sex, money, marriage, children, and religion satisfy the personal search for credibility and relevance offer unreliable promises. Yes, the aforementioned can be sources to achieve social credibility, but all such sources offer a legitimacy that is fundamentally conditional: therefore, unreliable and unsustainable.

Prominence and stature can disappear without prior warning within a system of living primarily based on attaining external and material value for purposes of credibility. Also, as time elapses within this system, physical beauty and sex become zero-valued commodities, children grow into distant satellites where communication lines are imaginary, marriage exposes two total strangers hanging out in the same locale, and orthodox religion continues to expect more compliance and tithes from its followers. Without the education and development of a person's inherent merits of character to establish genuine personal value, the gamble that emerges when pursuing credibility through various replicas creates difficult odds to overcome.

Putting his or her eggs into baskets with little to no staying power with the hope of achieving an externally based credibility and relevance can be a risky affair. Primary relationships, which include marriage, romance, siblings, and children are sources that receive enormous sums of emotional, psychological, and physical investments. The same can said for relationships of a secondary nature, which can include divorced parents, in-laws, coworkers, and close friends. The instinctual need to feel relevant is one of two essential motivational elements that contribute to the heavily emphasized emotional, psychological, and physical expectations that take place in both primary and secondary relationships. A need to feel credible is another element that can heighten expectations. With the personal investment ranking fairly high, it is wise to have a backup plan if and when the specific relationship fails to provide the much-anticipated credibility and relevance.

Whether the external and material world disappoints or not, having achieved an authentic and balanced personal value through character development offers the opportunity to define his or her legitimacy by more than experiences. Again, the option to fall back on an individuality preserved by good character is not a bad idea to seriously consider. Within a system of living that elevates external and material value above the innate value of an individual, the only manner in which an individual can define his or her credibility and relevance is through experiences. In addition, such a system of living makes it quite attractive to insert an external source into a position of being responsible for another person's well-being. Without question, this is an unsafe and treacherous accommodation factor to take on for both parties.

Even with the full knowledge that certain relationships are unsustainable and hazardous to a person's well-being, the need to feel relevant and credible can often override reason. Because a vacuum cannot exist within the human realm, self-importance and self-indulgence will fill the vacancy where the traits of good character would have normally existed. Immediate gratification, rather than patience and prudent thought, intercede to support self-interest. Minus an education and development of good character, self-importance and self-indulgence emerge well disguised to give an impression that credibility and relevance have justly been established. Because of this deficiency, inequities and inequalities usually materialize with one main purpose in mind, and that is to create divisions among people on the basis of superiority and inferiority. As expected, class, race, ethnicity, gender, religion, and politics are used to accomplish this historical agenda.

For the individual or group sitting in the catbird seat of privilege based on *what* he or she is externally and possesses materially, a sense of lack stimulated by greed will be the motivation to pursue power or more power. When superiority seeks to fulfill his or her desire to attain such markings that depict credibility and relevance, pursuits of this nature are aided by a distorted perception of entitlement. Dominance holds fast to a belief that it is quite appropriate to take from whomever or whatever to guarantee a desired end result. Since the pursuit for superiority is motivated by lack and fueled by greed and entitlement, what is attained through manipulation amounts to nothing more than securing a false sense of security. And just like an addict, once the euphoria begins to wear thin, repetition of an old habit takes center stage. The act of satisfying what in reality is an authentic and instinctual need to experience credibility and relevance begins all over again with attaining more false securities.

The constant search for bliss with its unpredictability, rather than actuality with its consistency and stability, will continue to be a source for personal disappointments. Nothing external can, in truth, satisfy an internal longing for the genuine. Educate to the merits of character and the thirst for the authentic is naturally, not artificially, fulfilled. However, due to a deficiency regarding the education of good character, priorities are turned upside down. The devotion to "the end justifies the means," rather than "the means justifies the end," takes precedence. The person or group sitting in the catbird seat of privilege within a system of living that recognizes external and material value as sole points of credibility are viewed as viable examples to follow.

Achieving power and dominance are given enormous impor-tance in order to attain credibility. And with character development missing from the educational landscape, broad segments of humanity pursue the same distortion fueled by the identical presumed entitle-ment. Marriages, romantic relationships, dictators, terrorists, ethnic cleansing, racial discrimination, religions, economic and financial manipulations that advance a tiny fraction of the populace serve as prime examples of pursuits in search of a false sense of security to claim a false position of superiority. Again, when a negative is used in the attempt to prove a positive, the net result is a negative, and yet, humanity continues to struggle with and clash unsuccessfully against its principled soundness.

Comparison will be the weapon of choice to use by an individual or group for the purpose of reinforcing his or her position of weakness or inferiority. Rather than take responsibility to help effect personal change, it is more desirable to focus on what others have in terms of external and material advantages. By using comparison, the individual or group can also solidify his or her position of victimhood. Educate to the strength and value of character and the weapon of comparison that can ultimately lead to incorporate acts of brutality and corruption to effect change is cast aside. The discovery that there is no need to take on the same oppressive behavior as the powerful is what makes genuine change a strong possibility.

However, when either lack or comparison becomes a dominant attitude, an attractive way to remedy this condition is to declare some form of warfare on another person or group. Both white- and blue-collar crimes stem from the superiority and inferiority mind-set. One-up and one-down relationships are easily forged together in this manner, as are the various forms of economic, racial, ethnic, political, religious and social bias and intolerance. The lack of education and development of character that is merit based provides an individual with the opportunity to assemble personal qualities that encourages deception to be part of his or her lifestyle. This form of deception occurs when portraying respect for another person or group that looks persuasive, but is shallow and lacks conviction.

This form of respect is developed to appear believable and genuine. At the time regard is verbally or nonverbally expressed, this same individual can maintain the belief that the specified individual or group lacks credibility and relevance. The pretense of respect is a natural occurrence that arises within a system of living that attaches credibility to external and material achievements more than it does to inherent credibility. This patronizing use of respect is obvious when credibility and relevance become intertwined with economic, racial, ethnic, religious, social, and educational inequities and inequalities. Again, where such practices exist, this behavior comes into play when a person is being addressed in a respectful manner, but is also being viewed as lacking credibility and relevance.

The belief that people are expected to live together in a civil manner regardless of the inequities and inequalities that are revolving throughout the landscape are what promotes patronizing respect as a feasible option for engagement. Preserving power, authority, and prominence are the motivations to deny legitimacy and importance to another individual or group deemed of lesser importance but appear opposite the intention to dominate. Relationships occurring within the circles of sameness and familiarity are also subject to this deceptive use of respect. Within families, primary relationships, racial, ethnic, and religious groups, the practice of patronizing respect takes place as a common occurrence. Without the recognition of the person beyond *what* he or she is externally and materially, the lack of credibility and relevance regarding that individual or group will become a major characteristic of the relationship.

Qualities such as intelligence, passions, creativity, perceptions, intuition, and ingenuity are important to notice in family, friends, and strangers, if credibility and relevance are to be genuinely accepted. For this reason alone, special attention is given to understanding the difference between the external display of respect and acknowledgment of inherent credibility through attributes that help define one's personage. Within a system of living overshadowed by external and material acclaim as a primary form of achieving credibility and relevance, the type of respect ushered about is conditional. Insert the education to substantive character, and credibility is discovered to be the opposite: unconditional. What starts out at the beginning of the day as a robust and serious ambition to be good and to do good ends up, at its conclusion, nothing more than a wishful contemplation.

Thought to be an attainable goal is the practice of acceptable standards of behavior toward individuals from different economic, political, social, and religious backgrounds. Civility is a way of life many people living in a mostly civilized world are eager to claim. Yet, to be good and to do good are two extremely difficult goals to accomplish throughout any given day, not to mention on a consistent basis. Achieving such altruistic goals are incredibly challenging to accomplish, and basically against the odds of succeeding. This, even in a civilized world populated by individuals who reject any notion of being a closeted or self-proclaimed autocrat.

How can it be any different when authority and prestige are based on conditional and unsustainable standards? How can it be any different when humanity refuses to recognize the intrinsic nature and value of human life? How can there be an honest moment of civility when accountability, vulnerability, and transparency are feared and held as contemptible attributes? Because such traits are viewed as signs of weakness, human interactions are consumed with wasting so much valuable time saying what is not meant and seeking from one another what he or she refuses to give to the other.

What is permissible to use as valid reasons that impede the practice of being good and to do good are two obstacles, which are neither complicated nor confusing to grasp. Both are by-products that represent a patchwork effort to conceal an inadequate development of character. Self-importance and self-indulgence are the two obstacles that prevent concluding the day with a personal goal to be good and to do good. The absence of an education, development, and practice of a person's attributes of admirable character makes it virtually impossible to execute the acts to be good and to do good with conviction and on a consistent basis.

Perfection is not needed for personal achievement, since accountability and transparency are components of character development. Without it, to assist and support the economic and social advancement of a person or group representative of a different background is extremely difficult to achieve. Civility is an easy intellectual concept to grasp when there is no personal perception that the individual or group representing a different background will advance his or her standing beyond the status quo. This is especially true within a system of living that solely values *what* an individual is externally and possesses materially.

Again, because credibility and relevance are equated with power within this system of living, the best that can be offered as a reward in terms of human engagements is an imitation of respect that is patronizing. There is nothing in play that is genuine when a person or group can elevate his or her societal position based on inequities and inequalities that manufacture external and material successes. It matters not that a morning goal is to be good and to do good when a way of life inspires a person to impersonate as best as he or she can the act of decency.

This is precisely the situation when personal value based on *what* an individual is externally and possesses materially become the defined margins for declaring credibility and relevance. Self-importance and self-indulgence derived from external and material prosperity make it an improbable act to recognize authentic personage and credibility of one's self, as well as another individual. This is especially true when the person or persons having the opportunity to do so has benefited from generations of economic, racial, ethnic, social, and religious advantages due to inequalities.

The endeavor is comparable to having a mental picture of what easy-over eggs, bacon, hash browns, and toast look like, but deficient in a practical sense how to transform the idea into an actuality. Since there is no profitability and personal gain attached to the altruistic act, economic, racial, ethnic, gender, and religious inequalities remain intact. In the case of another individual or group who represent a different and unfamiliar background, merely being a supportive witness to his or her moment of equality and equity is highly improbable: the stage has limited space. Where character development is a component of the educational process, to witness and support the equality and equity of another individual or group ensures the process includes the witness.

No longer is there a need to impersonate authentic credibility with patronizing respect, integrity with self-righteousness, and symbolic generosity with charitable donations. As previously stated, genuine authority is derived from the development and practice of his or her merits of character. This, added to an individual's internal portfolio, provides the opportunity to define oneself by more accurate and substantive information than limiting and oftentimes misleading personal experiences. And just as important, the opportunity is there to avoid creating a necessity to rely on self-importance and self-indulgence. Both qualities are considered major contributors to a distorted version of authority.

A widely used display of distorted authority occurs when a person or group has been repeatedly victimized by acts of cruelty that originate from a hostile and dominant force. The distorted authority materializes when the common strategy for retaliation against cruelty is comprised mainly of violent behavior. Rhetoric composed of anger and hatred precipitates the retaliatory action. Though the victimized are seeking what are considered appropriate reactions through violence, ultimately, the retribution undermines the legitimacy of the grievance. The lack of integrity will never bring to justice the lack of integrity.

History reveals how the success experienced by Mahatma

Gandhi, the Reverend Martin Luther King Jr., Jackie Robinson, and Rosa Parks was won by a nonviolent approach to legitimate grievances based on integrity. A positive will always bring a positive conclusion when the underpinning is a principled approach, whereas, for a brief moment, hostility and unbridled power may relieve anguish but assume the same position of oppression as the oppressor, nullifies the possibility of sustainable gains. The only sure gain to manifest itself under such conditions is the formation of more anguish and torment, which brings to fruition: "the more things change, the more they remain the same."

Besides, retaliation that is exhibited strictly through violence eventually runs its course, at which point the destructive behavior is directed inward. The initial pursuit of a righteous grievance will lose its focus and intensity when the energy propelling the complaint is lacking the core qualities of substantive character. Due to the absence of transparency, accountability, and vulnerability, unconstrained violence, in time, turns inward onto the offended individual or group the individual is most affiliated with in terms of economics, race, ethnicity, religion, or gender. After suicide bombs, mass killings, the burning of buildings, looting, ill-fated protests, and the psychoanalysis of young men, it is back to business as usual.

The infighting among Native Americans, African Americans, Muslims, women, and the elderly in the form of internalized discrimination and resentment are just a snapshot of groups divided within their own ranks. To discredit and even to destroy one another is the ultimate tragedy of this specified activity. Acts of brutality and crime committed within the respective factions perpetuate the condition of impoverishment and maintain a culture of professional victims. It is of interest to note how the internalized disdain held within the various factions is considered tolerable within a nation, family, ethnic, or religious group, but not when initiated from outside sectors.

Within a system of living that excessively emphasizes the external value of an individual, understating his or her inherent value leaves only one option to define credibility and relevance. Depending on his or her personal encounters with inequities and inequalities, the narrow window of experiences will be the determinant for credibility and relevance, or its lack. Rather than the inherent value attached to the qualities of good character determining legitimacy and importance, experiences that are either good or bad determine self-worth and personal value.

Again, when a man, woman, and child are educated to the best attributes he or she has to offer in this life, which are the traits of meritorious character, an overused pathway to self-identification is removed. Professional victimhood, as well as privilege and entitlement, is no longer a viable option for using the loosely woven credibility and relevance attached to personal experiences. Choosing to take on a belief system that supports a superior/inferior premise will generate distinct forms of distorted authority designed to produce conclusions that result in who is worthy and unworthy.

Religion, with its vast global influence, could help rectify this dilemma by taking more of an innovative approach to the issue of personal redemption. This new approach would begin with a commitment to teach a far more personalized form of redemption. Educate to the development and practice of an individual's inherent value as brought forth through his or her merits of character. When religion relies on rigid adherences, such as committing to memory articles of faith, tenets, doctrine, rituals, and obligatory attendance to induce compliance that is, in turn, rewarded with approval and external value, the outcome is predictable. Personal redemption is more about external glorification, rather than credibility and relevance based on inherent value.

This is one reason why religions are constantly attempting to outdo one another with respect to the number of converts during any given month. There is more glory attached to what religion a person may belong to, rather than acclaim for the universal wisdom that every man, woman, and child is of equal credibility and relevance based on his or her inherent value. Make no mistake, though limited, there is value in the personal declaration of being a Christian, Jew, Muslim, Catholic, atheist, or to any other religious faction. However, there is greater individual value in living the universal wisdom that honorable and meritorious character brings to the human condition, both on a personal and interpersonal level. Distinguished credibility and sustainable relevance offers substantial individual meaning and purpose.

Educate to the inherent value a person brings to his or her life and all religions are united as one in support of a system of living that understands the ultimate credibility and relevance to be the sanctity of human life. One religion is no better than the next when united under the banner of preaching and teaching the qualities of good character. There is no need to fear the devil, Satan, Beelzebub, Lucifer, the Prince of Darkness, or the Evil One when individuality is free to experience the kingdom within that represents the principle of good. There is no need to support the notions that a person is born into sin when entering this life, death is a better option than taking responsibility to live, or this world is governed and controlled by evil. All such ideas nullified when the innate value of good character is the vanguard for the distinction of personage.

This innovative approach to personal redemption would be a realistic way to maintain a moral balance between *what* a person is externally and possesses materially in relation to *who* he or she is regarding intrinsic value. Continuing to reinforce methods that focus on achieving personal redemption by developing a fundamental loyalty that glorifies *what* an individual is externally and materially accomplishes one end goal. The objective achieves nothing more than to perpetuate a long-standing personal *holy war* . . . the struggle whether to honor a credibility and relevance constructed on a house of cards or to honor what is built by the brick and mortar of substantive character. When emotional and spiritual impoverishment are left undisturbed by an intrusion of what is the best an individual can bring to his or her life, which are the attributes of good character, activity of a contrary nature takes place. A breeding process begins to escalate, and depravity becomes an inevitable consequence.

Evil is always an outward expression of the attempt to discredit and even destroy credibility and relevancy by means of a perverted use of influence and power. Evil in its attempt to exert what is a distorted sense of superiority and importance will oftentimes find it necessary to destroy the sanctity of human life. Such antilife approaches further reveal a profound and firmly established wickedness. In short, evil is the result of a prolonged and acute state of emotional and spiritual impoverishment propelled by a perverse sense of self-importance and self-indulgence. And, it is for this reason that evil invariably destroys itself through acts of self-betrayal that emerge from that same deviant sense of self-importance and self-indulgence.

Evil driven by an internal state of impoverishment will continue to exist so long as the belief that it cannot be conquered or destroyed is maintained outside its existence remains. And when the evil of this world and its historical intrusion no longer exceeds the belief that it can be conquered, a dramatic shift in the course of human history will have occurred due to one significant moral development. The intrinsic nature of an individual's life would have come to be recognized as an indispensable resource that builds the cornerstone for sustainable moral authority and credibility. And that all-important inherent resource would consist of the merits of an individual's character. It is purportedly stated by Jesus in the Book of Thomas, Gnostic Gospels, "If you bring forth what is within you, what you bring forth will save you. If you do not bring forth what is within you, what you do not bring forth will destroy you."

The condition of impoverishment begins internally and is expressed externally due a lack of development and practice concerning the inherent value of one's merits of character. Regardless of external experiences, be it positive or negative, nothing need be internalized as worthy or unworthy, relevant or irrelevant due to being educated to the true value of an individual's life. Evil has, unfortunately, played a dominant role throughout humanity's history in terms of creating a living hell on this earth. Regrettably, this will continue to be a constant intrusion into this life on earth as it exceeds the belief it can be conquered. Evil's presence will be known and felt when the state of emotional and spiritual impoverishment dominates the human existence.

Teach a woman, man, and child what constitutes the absolute best that he or she has to offer as a person, which will primarily be identifiable qualities of commendable character, and others will have a more convincing and compelling reason to personally achieve moral authority. The individual is prepared to emotionally, intellectually, psychologically, and spiritually grasp where and how his or her true value is derived. This same individual is empowered to consistently exercise good judgment with respect to establishing relationships that acknowledge the existence of qualities comprising a person's intrinsic nature.

Another important factor is the willingness to accept the relevancy and credibility of other people where differences, such as class, race, ethnicity, religion, politics, social position, and gender, may exist. Neglect this education regarding the development of good character and the individual, knowingly or unknowingly, agrees to take part in a disconcerting process that establishes credibility primarily on external criteria. Unsettling, because the inevitable letdown and anguish for colluding with a way of life that fails to consider or take into account the true value and intrinsic nature of the individual is just over the horizon.

Again, the accepted and sometimes disguised self-contempt will seek to express itself through a distorted sense of power and authority.

Unable to execute a genuine form of empowerment and authority outside the familiarity of experiences, the internalized inadequacy is left with no other choice than to turn on what is well known: itself. "I am what I experience and no more" is the tormented cry that can be heard from the mouths of highly professionalized victims. The powerful and dominant have remained as such throughout history because of the divide-and-conquer technique. Keep the different factions of people distracted by fighting among themselves over the issues of credibility and relevance, and oppression can be executed quite easily over the collective mass. This is precisely how inequities and inequalities can continue to flourish undeterred and uninterrupted. Fighting over who is superior and inferior will continue to add another unfortunate chapter to humanity's historical refusal to accept the value of the education and development of substantive character.

As a result of this refusal, lost is the opportunity to establish a nation, community, and family systems where conscious awareness is a priority. Hence, personal value primarily sought through external and material sources will continue to be the fuel that propels the unjust treatment of people based on class, economic, race, ethnic, religious, gender, education, and age differences. The refusal to accept the education and development of substantive character as a means to achieve genuine credibility and relevance also encourages an individual to continue to be defined by his or her experiences. This system of living will remain the only game in town.

As stated previously, the repercussions are always consistent when basically pursuing credibility from sources having limits and failings. Again, when a person allows his or her value to be defined by external sources, which include experiences that are good, bad, or indifferent, a personal declaration is made quite clear. That individual who capitulates to an impersonal source for credibility and relevance is making an admission and has accepted that he or she has no idea of how to live his or her own life.

Personal values and decisions that are formed actually represent dictates handed down from talking heads and talking points other than from his or her self. Clarity is further disclosed that any source responsible for providing credibility and relevance for another person or group has an incredible amount of manipulative power over that individual or group. The lack of a foundation comprising meritorious character means that deception, duplicity, and insincerity will dominate any prospect of achieving credibility and relevance. When the attainment of power and authority are the recognized measurements for success within a system of living preoccupied with external and material value, one certainty is a given reality. Prominence achieved through marriage, parenthood, companionship; the workplace; entertainment; race, ethnicity; religious, political, and civic groups offer finite and contingent forms of external credibility.

From one generation to the next, the harmful effects of focusing mainly on external resources for purposes of credibility are never questioned or rejected as unacceptable. Rugged individualism is never questioned as a contradiction to the true meaning of community. Therefore, people living or working in a close proximity of one another or having specific characteristics in common, such as the working and middle class, carry very little to no meaning. The exception occurs when one group of people are pitted against another group in terms of credibility and relevance, even if fabricated or distorted.

Affirmative Action, abortion, the disproportionate incarceration of African Americans, and whether to say "Merry Christmas" or "Happy Holidays" are wedge issues created to divide people who share more common interests than differences. The divisiveness has to do with the resistance or refusal to extend one's self to another individual for nothing more than the humane gesture of recognizing his or her credibility and relevance. The lack of interest or support in acknowledging another person's inherent importance who lives outside his or her circle of familiarity can be traced to a constricted system of living.

Maneuvering for positions of superiority and legitimacy while taking advantage of inequalities and inequities; class, race, ethnicity, religion, and gender become wedge issues, as well. Personal value solely defined by *what* an individual is externally and possesses materially is a product of an imbalanced system of living. To negate and not include the credibility and relevance of inherent value as brought forth by the merits of character as a major component for defining personal value is to breed corruption within this same system of living.

However, what brings this corruption to a dead end is the unthinkable. The disillusionment that eventually takes place when the bliss that accompanies credibility and relevance based on external sources runs its course with inevitability. Given the intrusion of time, the marriage, the special love relationship, physical appeal, identification with race, religion, career, children, house, and automobile all fail to provide the necessary importance and legitimacy previously attained. People change, and so do fluctuating and unstable standards. For this reason, it is unwise to primarily invest in external and material sources for purposes of achieving personal credibility and relevance.

Remorse can be an excellent motivator to summons from within accountability, transparency, vulnerability, and personal responsibility for purposes of redemption. This allows ownership to take place regarding the disinterest or disdain demonstrated toward the sanctity of human life during the pursuit of externa land material-based credibility. The personal acknowledgment of the people who were hurt and disregarded in order to satisfy the selfish want can be a huge step toward redemption and self-forgiveness. Coming face-to-face that all such pursuits were based entirely on self-importance and self-indulgence can open the inner door to experience humility.

However, the most challenging step toward redemption involves the act of forgiveness for the betrayal and unworthiness directed at one's self. Ignorance of the truth about one's self cannot be an excuse for the acts of self-betrayal.

But, it can be a valid reason toward understanding the state of impoverishment that held an immoral grip on his or her individuality. This to the extent the individual could not learn of and bring forth the best that he or she had to offer one's self and others: the strength and merits of character. The anguish associated with the realization of having internalized, through experiences, to view genuine attributes as of little worth to accommodate a deceptive and fickle external value system can be enough to motivate personal change. To serve a system of living by negating the best of honorable character, to later be denied credibility and relevance, deserves no further allegiance. Not measuring up to external values that are manipulated and quickly evaporate due to age, loss of physical appeal, and usefulness actually becomes a positive revelation.

Also coming from self-examination, a person can come to realize how the act to undermine or destroy another individual or group's credibility and relevance actually damages or destroys his or her own legitimacy; most often to a greater degree. To assume a position of entitlement due to attaining a status of personal distinction and superiority that occurred by taking advantage of social, religious, and educational inequities and inequalities is nothing short of deceit. And to act as though the credibility and relevance bestowed is earned, which perpetuates a presumption of dominance over factions of people manipulated to achieve such distinction, is a disgrace. Any economic, social, religious, and educational achievements disallowed to any one person or group due to economics, race, ethnicity, religion, gender, or age discrimination, while another is free to pursue without restrictions makes a mockery of integrity.

The disregard for credibility and relevance of another person or group becomes yet an additional point to address during the period of redemption. This is one reason why written or verbal histories under the control of the powerful and dominant will attempt to conceal the blatant acts to destroy the legitimacy of individuals and groups considered irrelevant. To acknowledge the legitimacy of individuals and groups once thought to be insignificant is an important step toward personal redemption. Introspective thought in conjunction with self-examination can be an excellent path to travel in terms of committing to a process to seek more reliable sources to achieve credibility and relevancy.

First of all, there is valuable information to draw upon that will help an individual learn the vast difference between credibility and respect. Learning the difference between doing what is good versus doing what is right, and saying what a person means to state versus saying what he or she thinks is appropriate to say, helps to differentiate between credibility and respect. Being polite, courteous, and donating to charities can be acts of respect that lack the recognition of inherent credibility for either the provider or recipient. Such choices have been made for the purpose of doing what is right but are motivated by self-interest. The Machiavellian rule to pretend to do right but engage in its opposite in order to maintain power and dominance remains in vogue.

Rather than continue submitting to unrepentant external sources to be personally defined, the road to learning and developing his or her merits of character can begin immediately. Better to develop a moral conscience through the acknowledgment of substantive character than to forgo this process in favor of immediate gratification. To leave the road most traveled for the road less traveled reduces the negative impact self-importance and self-indulgence can create due to the state of impoverishment. Again, educate to the merits of character, and empty words attached to a conditional acceptance will no longer be accepted as a means to achieve what turns out to be nothing more than a dubious form of credibility. Instead, in its place, the individual gladly recognizes inherent legitimacy after having learned where and how sustainable credibility and relevance is derived.

However, on the flip side of this viewpoint remain individuals and groups completely opposed to the idea of inherent credibility and relevance. There are people thoroughly invested in the concentration of power, passion, authority, and intelligence being in the hands of one or just a few, which are indications of a personal agenda that involves empire building. The ability to accomplish this goal and maintain one's position of superiority exists for one reason. Those individuals under their control are lacking the knowledge of the gifts of character, and therefore, are in dire need to experience relevancy and credibility.

And thus, words promising a greener pasture outside of his or her personage will carry a greater meaning than the development of his or her attributes of good character that can establish a coalition of equals. To reach the depth of sound character where such qualities as integrity and mutuality are forged together to have more of a legitimate meaning, engaging with the unfamiliar, are excellent means to achieving this goal. Whereas, remaining close to sources that breed familiarity and contingent credibility keeps the meaning of such qualities merely esoteric and intellectual.

Diversity has its advantages when it comes to moving the comfort zone beyond the familiar in anticipation of developing moral character. This is especially true when one is faced with extending qualities of character that constitute depth, such as transparency, accountability, and mutuality to a person or group regarded as different in terms of class, race, ethnicity, politics, religion, or gender. Wisdom teaches the humble that it is impossible to achieve the best for one's self, and at the same time, ignore, deny, or destroy the opportunity for another to achieve his or her best. Social contracts not resembling a coalition of equals but are designed to function as autocratic and arbitrary in due course become problematic when under a mind-set preoccupied with self-importance and self-indulgence. When the two traits are the rule, there clearly is no room for another person or group.

For this reason, it is wise not to take into one's confidence an individual or individuals who do not share the same value when it comes to establishing a balance of power. And this is especially true when this balance of power is to achieve mutual credibility, authority, relevancy, intelligence, and vision. Where there is a difference when it comes to establishing a mutual balance of power versus a concentration of power, it is important to remember there will be consequences to pay. When this dissimilarity is disregarded as insignificant by the person invested in power, the assumption is made that he or she seeking mutuality will acquiesce in favor of accommodation.

When such a disparity is not taken into account when considering forming a relationship of importance, intimacy can later become a weapon, rather than an experience of bonding. For example, significant moments that are shared or information disclosed in private can be used in a mean-spirited manner to weaken and dishonor credibility by the advocate for a concentration of power. This, for the primary purpose of wielding a demanding form of power; one that is based on superiority and domination. The inability to exercise an adequate degree of self-protection, upheld by a refusal to recognize the difference, can have one result: acquiesce without protest.

After having taken into one's confidence a person or group opposed to mutuality, transparency, and accountability in order to establish credibility, it is disappointing to learn that the partner simply sought power and domination to control the relationship. But, this information only arrives after the novelty of the relationship's newness has become passé. One clearly cannot prove a positive from a negative when the value systems regarding credibility and relevance are so opposite of one another. When he or she is a proponent for a balance of power, to pursue recognition and importance from a proposed confidant who favors a concentration of power guarantees a negative outcome. A person educated to the merits of his or her character, which includes its intrinsic value, is steadfast with exercising good judgment not to seek approval and validation from extrinsic sources that are unpredictable and unreliable.

As a matter of fact, what is most known to occur when seeking confirmation and recognition from outside of oneself is the expectation of absolute compliance from that extrinsic source. Undoubtedly, this substantiates how the probability of being viewed favorably by the external source is persistently based on the terms of conditions. The phrase that best describes this type of relationship can be stated as thus: to seek from others what one refuses to give to others unless conditions of approval are satisfied beforehand. When the basis for seeking credibility from an external source is so compromised as to settle for conditional acceptance, the light at the end of the tunnel is nonexistent. There is no need to entertain any notion of a balance of power or a gathering of equals on the part of the proposed confidant who seeks a concentration of power.

If he or she is to enter into such an arrangement, to accept the directive that a person has to prove his or her worth in order to attain relevance, an unholy alliance with coercion is about to be established. Rather than accept the universal principle that it is never ever necessary to prove one's worth to achieve credibility, the lack of character development reveals a shortcoming. The need to pursue an association with a person or group that has no fear of using force or threats to strengthen its own self-importance and self-indulgence at the expense of the naïve discloses the weakness. The unholy alliance gains traction as evidenced by an individual's willingness to accommodate imbalance and inequity to gain the less-than-stable manufactured credibility. The eagerness to rush into a committed relationship or marriage with a virtual stranger simply because credibility is socially bestowed upon such endeavors stand as excellent examples of the absolute necessity to attain relevancy and importance.

Children giving birth to children is another example of the attempt to prove one's social gravity and weight, with the motivation being to demonstrate his or her importance as a parent for the purpose of achieving credibility and relevance. It is not surprising that interwoven into such a pursuit are well integrated discrepancies identifiable as deception, manipulation, and coercion. An earlier statement bears repeating; when a negative is used in the attempt to prove a positive, the net result is always a negative. The endeavor to prove to an external source an individual's credibility, rather than simply living his or her relevance based on the acceptance of intrinsic value, sets in motion for the opposite to occur. Again, the pursuit to accommodate any external source will never be enough to achieve a balance of power, nor reliable credibility and relevance.

The inability to understand intrinsic value and its stability is what drives a person to expend a great amount of effort and energy proving what has no need to be proven . . . just lived. It simply is never necessary to prove to anyone what is already in place and praiseworthy on its own merit, which substantive character has on its own. When the practice of his or her merits of character is a dominant way of life, recognition and relevancy of such attributes are what generate self-fulfillment. It is far better to be good than to be right. It is far better to be good than to be number one. It is far better to be good than to manipulate others for the sake of attaining credibility and relevance.

A way of life that principally values *what* an individual is externally and possesses materially also has the power to pronounce an individual unworthy and lacking in both validation and credibility. Not measuring up to external values unrelated to the human essence are the determining factors. Development and practice of an individual's merits of character guarantees he or she does not have to spend time proving to external sources what it cannot appreciate: personage.

In conclusion, the attempt to prove out a false positive in relation to economic, social, political, religious, race, ethnic, gender, and physical superiority for the purpose of inflating importance and seeking an advantage over others is simply to prove a negative. Regardless of self-serving traditions, doctrine, and spin, manufactured credibility that is based on criteria other than the qualities of good character are nothing more than an attempt to define a false positive as a genuine article. The endeavor to prove a positive through means that undermine civility and integrity can only produce a negative conclusion, no matter how seemingly valuable the gain.

Because there is an absence of qualities such as accountability, transparency, mutuality, and personal responsibility, a moral vacuum is created, which renders the chance of achieving credibility based on an ethical process an impossibility. To help ensure that the transition into the manufactured credibility is as seamless as possible, satisfaction with the outcome is frequently exaggerated and often verbally expressed to justify using the misguided rationale—the end justifies the means.

However, such a personal satisfaction devoid of substance can develop the basis for an unethical mind-set that can be quite lasting. For example, except when the sacredness of life pertains to one's self, very little, if any, appreciation for the sanctity and credibility of human life as it pertains to others is deemed worthy of recognition and value. And this is especially true where differences are apparent. It is virtually impossible to recognize and value the reasoning—the means justify the end—without first being exposed to the education and development regarding one's own composite of meritorious character. When the substance of character has been allowed to emerge, the means will have offered a natural and uncomplicated arrival at personal wholeness and completeness. Without question, the end can reflect a complex individual, but not marked by confusion and difficulty with understanding the person.

If not during the present generation, certainly lying in wait for later generations to struggle with is the ill-fated inheritance passed on that has absolutely nothing to do with riches and material wealth. The bequest has more to do with passing on a legacy ripe for creating a condition of emotional and spiritual impoverishment. Rather than pass on the blueprint for the growth of personal empowerment as discovered through character development, a nagging proverb is handed off: "the more things change, the more they remain the same." The age-old models of shrewd or devious influences, oppression, and cruelty used to achieve a manufactured credibility and relevancy that keep humanity chained to a state of impoverishment remain in fashion. These same methods used by past generations become the identical methods that will be employed by subsequent generations to achieve power and domination.

Adding insult to injury, this same extrinsic value is then catapulted to a position explicitly to imply a superiority over others, whereby handcrafted doctrine and dogma are then created to substantiate this lofty status. As long as intrinsic value is deemed to be of less credibility than nationalistic pride, political ideology, religious dogma, economic conceit, physical vanity, ethnic and racial superiority, the sanctity of human life will be left with no other fate than to be diminished in favor of self-importance and self-indulgence. Intrinsic value as it pertains to the inherent gifts of meritorious character elevates the sacredness of human life to a conscious level. This after having discovered that nothing associated within this life can offer the sustainability afforded the most sacred relationship: the individual and his or her gifts of character.

Chapter Five

STRENGTH OF CHARACTER OR IMPOTENCY

"*All dysfunction is ultimately rooted in impotency. A perception of impotency is an internalized sense that one has insufficient control over a particular aspect of his or her life. This perception has a tendency to manifest itself in unexpected ways. For example, when an individual feels he or she lacks control in a specific area of his or her life, an irrational desire for perfection can manifest itself in that person's work or relationships. Racism, classism, sexism, eating disorders, alcoholism, drug addiction, homophobia, and work obsession are all symptoms of an individual's own insecurities or perceived lack of control. Control and power are often the remedies sought by those who feel impotent.*"

Luke Turpeinen

A tired soul was once overheard saying, "Enough is enough." That same tired soul must have said a short time later in response to a re-occurrence of the absurd, "The more things change, the more they remain the same." This monotonous, disheartening, and repetitious history that humanity is vehemently committed to reproducing on a daily basis because of a refusal to advance beyond an accepted internalized state of impotency challenges its continued and credible existence. The inability to appreciate and value the sanctity of human life has now become an obvious and enormous impediment to its moral advancement. Moral clarity, discipline, and fortitude have become comic like abstractions, as opposed to meaningful values to develop and live by, as humanity's dreaded obsessions to debase, devalue, and destroy one another become the accepted norm. Thus, any serious attempt to value the sacredness of human life is overshadowed and sacrificed in favor of the indiscretions created by self-serving interest.

The Austrian novelist Marie von Ebner-Eschenbach once stated, "In youth we learn; in age we understand." What is it that we learn in youth that necessitates us to understand with age? What compels an individual to take the initiative to understand in age that what has been learned in youth is simple: a troublesome history of disappointments, failures, and mistakes that were never intended to occur. In youth, we learn that we can fall in love at thirty-five miles an hour, standing in the checkout line at the neighborhood grocery or during a casual stop at the office water cooler.

With age, we understand that any attempt to fill an internal void or longing primarily through external and material resources has a definite outcome of never being enough to satisfy the emptiness. To force an experience to take place on the pursuit for fulfillment, such as marriage, having children, or purchasing that dream home or automobile, can also create painful despair. The mind-set, *I want what I want when I want it,* can never take the place of learning to live within a process of evolution and preparation if sustainable success is to be achieved.

In youth, we learn that youth is everlasting and to take this idea for granted. In age, we learn of the impermanence of human life and the discretion to never take that idea for granted. In age, we learn that the only sustainable and worthy credibility and authority an individual can lay claim to is that credibility and authority he or she came into this life with: the inherent gifts of character. Integrity, community, generosity, and civility are invaluable to building constructive relationships, whereas, in youth, we learn that credibility and relevance are primarily achieved through the domination, manipulation, and deception of other people. In youth, it is what an individual is externally and materially that matters above all else. Paradise, contentment, fulfillment, and completion are all externally and materially based. The end justifies the means, and immediate gratification is what pushes this viewpoint to center stage.

In youth, we learn to prey upon the illusions of one another for selfish gain because we have learned quite well that destinations such as contentment, fulfillment, completion, and bliss are all externally and materially within a fingertip grasp. Hence, "survival of the fittest" becomes a fight song to inspire the youth . . . provided an individual is fortunate to live beyond the consequences of decisions and choices based principally on self-importance and self-indulgence, complexity moves to the top of the list of personal admiration replacing the accumulating complications one has naïvely created. Typically revealed through physical and emotional illness, long-term anguish, death, or a rigid denial to keep intact the status quo, in age, an individual has the opportunity to fully understand how complexity reveals the depth and layers of one's individuality. Always based in good, integrity, community, and generosity, individuality opens the door to appreciating complexity because it reveals who the individual is intrinsically in terms of meritorious character.

When the value or diminished value of an individual is predominantly determined by external and material measurements, one predictable conclusion will occur during that individual's lifetime. Drama is added to the conclusion because this same individual was willing to consent to being valued by an unstable system, in the first place, through the various forms of compliance. The conclusion: He or she eventually deduces that so much has been given . . . for so little in return. As a result of compromising and shrinking individuality in order to comply with a value system that principally determines an individual's credibility and legitimacy by external and material measurements, an inevitable result is assured. The individual is encouraged by such a value system to accept an internalized perception of impotency. The same encouragement awaits the individual who simply lacks an education, understanding, and appreciation for the qualities of character. This perception that one is insufficient, inconsequential, deficient, and ineffective is eventually solidified by an acceptance of a state of emotional and spiritual impoverishment.

When individuality is strengthened and maximized by the implementation of the inherent gifts of character, there is no such occurrence as self-will. Impotency is nonexistent. Integrity, civility, patience, respect, passion, and community are not qualities shrouded in abstractions but in sensibility and genuine value. Conversely, when individuality is lacking the execution of the inherent gifts of character, self-will seeks immediate gratification, and impotency is cloaked in self-importance and self-indulgence.

Power, control, and a shift from personal responsibility for one's well-being to contracting out that responsibility to as many external and material sources deemed possible become the end game. Where there is a rigid denial structure in place to guard against the recognition and value ascribed to the inherent gifts of character, there is no reason to consider personal change. To have benefited from self-importance and self-indulgence through value determined by external and material measurements renders the qualities of substantive character insufficient and inconsequential.

Mired in a state of privilege or despair through consent to being valued or marginalized does not lend itself to taking advantage of an opportunity to examine through introspection what can be rightly understood from what has been learned erroneously. Moral clarity, discipline, and fortitude simply cannot exist nor have an opportunity to develop when an individual is willing to consent to having his or her value or diminished value primarily determined by external and material measurements. One of the most unsettling realizations, which amounts to the greatest cost extracted from an individual who fully buys into a way of life that primarily values *what* an individual is externally and materially is how so much is given for so little in return. Relentlessly pursuing a value system that is forever moving the goal posts of worth, always asking for more sacrifice, and in the end, simply cares so little about the individual's well-being accomplishes one sure fact. Relinquishing individuality maximized by the merits of one's character leaves a very hungry and thirsty soul always seeking that which is never fully gratifying: the confirmation and validation from external sources.

In youth, we learn that what is right is good, and very little to no action is required to accomplish what is demonstratively good. In age, we learn that what is good is always right, but what is right is not necessarily good. When what is right will benefit one side of the tracks but not the other, such as setting free a slave community into a culture where the apparatus of racism was very much intact, the right move is not necessarily a good move. Affirmative Action was a right move to make in thinning out the dominant effects of gender and racial discrimination, thus encouraging women and African Americans to enter the education and employment markets in greater numbers. However, it was not necessarily a good move to make while doing nothing to move the implementation of this corrective measure beyond the specter of what an individual is externally, such as being a woman or an African American. For women and African Americans to expand on the capacity to benefit from this measure, and for the white American male not to view this action as some privilege and entitlement bestowed upon the two groups, a significant event needed to occur prior to this measure being enacted.

What would have sent a powerful message to all Americans was that this measure was more than just about what the two groups were externally. Implementing this social change was an opportunity to enhance who we were as Americans, because such a shift would be based on the principle of integrity as well advancing the entire nation toward moral clarity. Understandably, naïveté on the part of this writer is unwarranted here. For this act to have occurred, it would have meant that this type of information and education had previously been practiced throughout the American culture, and it simply was not.

For an act of good to qualify as good, the deed has to impact the lives on both sides of the tracks. The tide will lift all boats when an act of good is executed, while an act of what is right but not necessarily good will lift only one or two boats at a time. Approval of the Nineteenth Amendment of the United States Constitution, which granted women the right to vote just in time to participate in the presidential election of 1920, was both a good and right measure to implement. It's absurd to have a document, such as the United States Constitution, which was meant to represent and uphold the dignity of every individual living within its democracy while disallowing the voice of American women to be heard.

And thanks to the American Civil Rights Movement, an identical argument can be made when the United States Congress passed the Voting Rights Act of 1965, which gave African Americans and poor white Americans full enfranchisement. The tide lifted all boats with this decision—both a good and right measure to implement into the American culture. It is an extremely difficult task not to internalize a perception of impotency when an individual is denied a credible voice in his or her nation, culture, family, religion, place of employment, or primary relationships. The same is true for the individual who is in a position of power and denies other individuals under his or her authority a legitimate voice: impotency is difficult to overcome under such conditions.

Ineffective, insufficient, and lacking are feelings quite difficult to triumph over, unless an individual has been educated to recognize the value and substance of his or her inherent gifts of character. Impotency or its mere suggestion is simply viewed as a dead carcass along the roadside. The recurrence of the absurd continues to materialize in the form of housing, Wall Street, Dot-com bubble, recession, and income gap crisis to sit historically alongside a National Depression, denial of a woman's right to vote as well as to receive equal pay, slavery, and the subsequent racial injustices toward blacks.

In age, we do away with such nonsensical tactics to gain what amounts to frivolous advantages over one another because we have come to understand that we are indeed our brother and sister's keeper. This understanding arrives in age because we have also understood the exact and true meaning of the statement, "But for the grace of God, there go I." The call to action is not to take responsibility for my brother or sister's well-being, but to assist in teaching each how to fish for the sustenance that will support achieving that level of well-being. Preying upon the weakness and vulnerability of another only enslaves the perpetrator to his or her misguided illusions. Educating an individual on the merits of one's character safeguards my brother and sister's existence; this also safeguards the existence of the environment. Impotency on both sides of the tracks is reduced to yesterday's unlearned history, unfit to be repeated in a civilized world.

In youth, though we may appear civil externally, we are often anything but civil toward one another behind the scenes in primary relationships such as marriage, family, committed friendships, and closed relations where sexual interactions are involved. As the struggle for power and control is played out, the clash usually boils down to who will take on the role of master and who will acquiesce to the role of servant. The master has an agenda based on self-importance and self-indulgence, and it is the duty of the servant to help carry forth that agenda. Sex, companionship, and materialism are often used as tools to achieve submission.

What is often overlooked after such determinations have been made is that whoever accepts the role as servant in the relationship eventually revolts against the master and the imbalance in the relationship. In order to consent to follow a way of life that bases the primary value of an individual on external and material criteria, relationships must be structured on a one-up and one-down formula. Divorce is imminent, and mortal enemies are assured to occur unless the parties involved agree to restructure the relationship on the basis of a coalition of equals.

Systematically speaking, when relationships are formed based strictly on the value of *what* an individual is externally and materially, that way of life will intentionally establish a tier or class structure for self-aggrandizing and classification purposes. Tier one of the class structure is reserved for the very important. These individuals are in command of absolute power, holding prestigious positions, credentials, and excessive wealth. Tier two is reserved for the important. These individuals are mainly in support positions with respect to the very important. The closer one is to the top tier of unrestrained influence, the more prominent the support position.

However, the important individual can be depicted as having limited and well-defined power, titles that will resemble significance but are actually one-dimensional and narrow credentials. Tiers one and two make it necessary for tier three to exist: the marginal and expendable. Tier three is where the majority of humanity exists. To help maintain an emotive, fanatical, and dedicated tier three, those representing tiers one and two consistently put into play exhausted and longstanding divisive measures that will provoke animosity and infighting among tier-three inhabitants.

The economy, health care, housing crisis, corporate greed, out-sourcing of American jobs, unemployment, underemployment, im-migration, education, the environment, border security, war, racism, gay and lesbian marriage, minimum wage, Medicare, Medicaid, abortion, and crime are a sample of the many social issues tier three will eagerly wolf down like a 800-pound alligator prepared to launch itself upon a small morsel of food. Historically and currently, social issues used to create division and discord continue as an effective way to keep tier three occupied and distracted with small morsels rather than the bigger picture. All social issues arise due to the lack of moral clarity, discipline, and fortitude on both sides of the debate. A way of life focused predominantly on the external and material as the manner to determine credibility will lack all three measures of morality, simply because the principle of integrity will have been sacrificed for selfish gain: the precursor to impotency.

In age, we understand that when an individual develops faith and hope largely as a result of the value and credibility ascribed to what he or she is externally and materially, the condition of emotional and spiritual impoverishment is less intense and extreme. The overall value attributed to the merits of character is minimized, thereby establishing a condition of impoverishment. Credibility and value based primarily on external and material measurements necessitates that the merits of character, such as integrity, community, and gen-erosity, be set aside. In favor of self-importance and self-indulgence, control and one-dimensional authority must be exercised against subordinates in order to maintain a drive motivated by self-interest.

Again, moral clarity, discipline, and fortitude are endangered because relationships are based on conditions, rather than being unconditional and authentic. Impotency remains an internal issue because credibility and value are externally and materially estab-lished. Rather than being established through the recognition, value, and demonstration of the individual's inherent credibility through the merits of character, the unsustainable is relied upon for feeling relevant. An internalized perception of being insufficient, inadequate, and apprehensive, while appearing outwardly to be in complete control and powerful, can hardly withstand the test of time when moral clarity, discipline, and fortitude are considered inconsequential. What eventually brings an individual to his or her knees in a moment of shame and humiliation, hopefully, later to be replaced with self-respect and humility, is the understanding that values concerning morality have been replaced with self-importance and self-indulgence.

Not being emotionally and spiritually grounded with one's inherent gifts of meritorious character, an individual comes to believe that being in control and powerful replaces the internal perception that he or she is impotent. In youth, we learn to bring what we are externally and materially to what we do, whereas in age, we learn to bring who we are to what we do if we are serious and sincere about achieving a measure of protracted success. Relying too heavily on *what* we are externally and materially breeds an internal condition of impotency. The lack awareness, value, and demonstration of one's true identity and individuality will accomplish this feat. A coalition of equals is the greatest threat to a way of life primarily based on external and material value. Impotency, dependency, and a victim mentality are the measures that will maintain a tier three that will fight among itself for the alleged right to move up into tier two or one, a tier that has no true sense of its collective and individual empowerment.

To encourage and support such initiatives as educating an individual about the merits and value of one's character, which is where self-empowerment resides, is certainly out of the question. Tier three agrees to this dumbing down design because of its complete acceptance that the value of an individual is determined exclusively through external and material means. Purity, rivalry, and complete obedience to divisive measures designed to fracture and fragment tier three, such as religion, politics, class, race, and ethnicity, are routinely reinstituted to keep the populace at odds with one another. Nationalistic slogans, such as a right to achieve the American dream and the need to pass onto the next generation a better way of life are also measures that keep humanity distracted with worthless illusions.

As long as passing on to the next generation a better way of life and the American dream remain as ideas attached to immediate gratification, materialism, and the quantitative, the outcome is fairly obvious. Rather than both ideals being monitored and motivated by quality and character, greed, crisis, and overindulgence consume a human multitude intent on chasing an illusion that attempts to give credibility to the absurd.

The notion that external and material gratification will equate into a substantive realization is purely nonsensical. As age will reveal in due course, the opposite comes into realization through various forms of misfortune, such as economic recessions and depressions, Wall Street and corporate greed, banking crises, credit card abuse, unemployment, housing, and mortgage calamities. For the impotent, these are not difficult experiences to create, especially when they are primarily seeking the American dream through external and material means as a way to feel credible.

Greed, corruption, and living beyond one's financial means naturally will occur when self-importance and self-indulgence replace moral clarity, discipline, and fortitude. Either due to a lack of education or a total disregard for the inherent gifts of character, nationalistic slogans and philosophy simply cannot move beyond breathtaking, reverberating abstractions.

James Truslow Adams, the architect of the term, the American dream, stated in 1931, "Life should be better and richer and fuller for everyone, with opportunity for each according to ability or achievement." This became America's first and only national philosophy and slogan in which freedom included a promise of the possibility of prosperity and success. Adams's intention was to include every American within the scope of the dream, regardless of social class or circumstances of birth. It is of interest to note that the basis of the American dream is embedded in the United States Declaration of Independence. This founding document declared that "all men [and women] are created equal" and that they are "endowed by their Creator with certain inalienable Rights," which include "Life, Liberty, and the pursuit of Happiness." It is extremely difficult to imagine that Mr. Adams's original intent was to bury his American dream inside the tomb of external and material gratification. His ideal comes across as a statement of principle and unadulterated vision, rather than one intended for the purposes of greed and self-interest.

Perhaps the reason for the decline of such a statement of principle and unadulterated vision lies with an evident actuality. As this nation and the global community has moved since 1931 to further encase itself inside an external and material mausoleum, this country, and the rest of the world, has become a human dramatization where it is every man and every woman for him or herself. Succumbing to a way of life solely based on what an individual is externally and materially—absent moral clarity, discipline, and fortitude—will, unfortunately, produce such an outcome. The same humanity that Mr. Adams was speaking of, hopefully and eventually, will come to embrace the truth that we, with our multitude of distinct cultures, ethnicities, religions, levels of education, and politics, have so much to offer one another as a result of our diverse and rich backgrounds.

However, the probability of prosperity and success for humanity, in general, will depend greatly upon the recognition, value, and demonstration of the inherent gifts of meritorious character. In this way, impotency acted out through aggression, control, and deceit recede to the backdrop of the human landscape to take up a posture of unimportance. If the pursuit of prosperity and success does not commence with the principle of integrity as its broker to respect and protect the sanctity of the human experience, then this pursuit is akin to swimming with sharks that know all too well how to devour the human spirit. The solitary reason an individual would choose to swim with the sharks is the mistaken belief that he or she can skillfully serve two masters: that of deception and that of truth. The fact that the tranquil and often-blue seas can offer up an illusion of exhilaration to neatly coincide with self-importance and self-indulgence is of no surprise. Without integrity, contradiction is hard to detect.

In age, we understand that when an individual has lost faith and hope in what he or she is, in addition to the acute disconnect regarding who he or she is with respect to the inherent gifts of character, the effect is intense and extreme emotional and spiritual impoverishment. This represents tier four of the class structure humanity inevitably establishes for itself as it pursues a way of life based predominantly on what an individual is externally and materially. The outcome of such a state of impoverishment can create a likely situation where an individual will cause injury and harm to others, as well as to him or herself.

Navigating airplanes into buildings, horrific crimes of passion or outright suicide are simply not out of the realm of possibility. When such an extreme state of impoverishment exists, the individual will surrender to an internalized condition of impotency. Other forms of impotency that represent only a slightly less degree of extreme impoverishment, but still register injury to others and one's self, are as follows: addiction, depression, rape, rage and uncontrollable anger, infidelity, suicide bombing, genocide, terrorism, ethnic cleansing, racism, classism, sexism, ageism, adultism, homophobia, arrogance, entitlement, greed, poverty, and other forms of discrimination.

The one experience that humanity has accomplished and accomplished quite thoroughly is the inability to get along with one another. Whether the relationship is individual-to-individual, community-to-community, culture-to-culture, or nation-to-nation, the inability to demonstrate a basic level of respect for one another and an appreciation for the sanctity of human life is the one feat that has completely eluded the grasp of global and local relationships. Race, ethnicity, nationality, religion, politics, education, and economic differences have always been used as instruments to divide humanity and inspire animosity. A question that will remain an unsolved mystery is, "How is it that with so much in common, humanity would rather focus on the irrelevant differences?"

With age, if we are fortunate to survive the ominous consequences resulting from the choices and decisions made based on a lack of awareness regarding strength of character, we can learn that authentic credibility and authority are achieved through the personal exploits of integrity, community, generosity, and the practice of good. With age, we also learn that most, if not all, of what we learned in youth is to be unlearned because the choices and decisions made netted us only short-term gain and immediate gratification, as well as very little in terms of fulfillment and sustainable success.

We still go to bed hungry and thirsty, with the knowledge that we, just a few hours ago, ate an excellent meal and drank what amounted to a satisfying beverage. But, within two or three hours, we awake with a ravishing thirst and hunger that has absolutely nothing to do with wanting another meal or beverage. We awake with much of the same thoughts echoed by Raymond Hill, another young American aspiring for a career in politics. "Have you ever had that feeling, in the very pit of your stomach—that feeling of wanting so desperately to 'go home,' only to be overtaken with the poignant realization that you don't have any idea of where or when 'home' might have existed?" Individuality supported by the inherent gifts of an individual's character guarantees a place that he or she can call home. It is wise to remember that the kingdom is indeed within, which will be the strength and merits of his or her character.

Chapter Six

RESPECT OR CREDIBILITY

*"Better to write for yourself and have no public,
than to write for the public and have no self."*

Cyril Connolly

"Hell happens when the evil of this world exceeds the belief that we can conquer it." Either self-inflicted or inflicted by an external source, hell can be closely linked to personal anguish and torment. As is often the case, this agony and despair is revealed through external suffering, such as depression, drug and alcohol abuse, bulimia, anorexia, criminal activity, and isolation. When despondency becomes weighed down with one's personal sense of loss before the type of intervention that can help to reveal his or her true value, a state of impoverishment is thus created. Hell begins to internally breed upon itself when a person, either through a conscious or unconscious act, is totally detached from his or her inherent credibility.

It is important to learn and know that inherent credibility is the type of legitimacy not to be overlooked. As an essential element to establishing relevance without the use of deception and manipulation, this legitimacy can eliminate any form of impoverishment. Due to a lack of education and understanding with respect to this blueprint for credibility, the roots for meritorious character to develop and grow are not able to occur. The complication is further compounded when individuality is reined in for purposes of appeasement. This occurs in order to fit in with the wishes or needs of an external source positioned to grant approval. In point of fact, what is actually granted is a pretense of credibility disguised to look like respect.

When a person puts him or herself in a position to be defined and approved of by an external source, an important event will take place. The accommodation and performance model is offered up to the source with the hope of achieving credibility and relevancy. Rather than rely upon the qualities of good character to achieve this distinction, due to a lack of training to identify and trust such attributes, self-betrayal enters into the human experience. Emotional, intellectual, and spiritual impoverishment develops in place of personal empowerment, because the best representation a person can make on his or her behalf is denied legitimacy. The qualities of ethical character, a vital element to substantiating and improving the human experience, are set aside to accommodate and perform to the expectations of an external source. In terms of communicating, so much time and effort is devoted to saying what a person does not mean, and what he or she does mean to say to be authentic remains mute: complicity must be observed.

Instead of seeking commonality at the table of equality, allegiance is, instead, handed over to one or more systems of living that equate credibility with power and dominance. Whoever enjoys this form of credibility, in turn, has the authority to define relevance and irrelevance as it pertains to others. Class, race, ethnic, gender, political, religious, and age differences are exploited within each category of people, as well as outside the group. For unrestrained power and dominance, the sole purpose is to define who is relevant and who is irrelevant. This practice ensures that a system of living remains authoritative, and most of all, in a position to rule over other people. What takes precedence is a plan to dismantle and undermine the credibility of any person or group with different physical markings, systems of ideals and ideas. Because credibility and relevance are conditional, individuals within each grouping are expected to be in agreement regarding the downgrading of credibility for other people with differences, warranted or not. When efforts are made to elevate the credibility of its respective system of living, expectations are that there will be obliging support and solidarity.

Under such conditions of living, it is difficult to design and implement methods that teach the value and practicality of ethical character. Carefully crafted methods of deception that pit one classification of people against another also makes it difficult to detect when a person is in pursuit of credibility and relevancy solely based on self-interest. This difficulty with detecting duplicity is further complicated due to a predisposition by the naïve to confuse the pretense of respect to mean credibility. However, there are signs of this being a priority if an individual is willing to forestall his or her pursuit of self-interest. Discussions with another person or group holding different values and opinions are turned into exercises based on who is right, rather than an exchange of ideas. Other notable behaviors would include simply going along to get along, and seeking from others what he or she refuses to give to others.

The lack of regard for differences becomes the norm when impoverishment regarding the attributes of good character dominates self-perception. The anticipated effect is resurrecting self-importance and self-indulgence to levels of privilege and entitlement. History customarily records how hell happens because evil is an instrument for the impoverished to yield for the purposes of power. Upon falling under the seductive influence of self-importance and self-indulgence, evil becomes an accepted consequence. As for the external source positioned to approve or disapprove the credibility and relevancy of another, underneath the facade of a pretense of credibility is contempt. And why not, when such power to define another human being as worthy or unworthy, relevant or irrelevant has been so easily handed over. Literally speaking and in theory, the process is set to attach personal identity to a deceptive and unreliable external anchor.

Hopefully, as an individual grows in age and matures with the help of remorse and regret, he or she comes to grasp how this is a very risky proposition. Because credibility is conditional within a system of living that links legitimacy to external and material value, the risk is quite clear-cut. Legitimacy linked with the capability to accommodate and perform to the satisfaction of an external source creates conditions whereby ethical behavior is victimized for the sake of a desired end result. Economic, social, political, and religious institutions can attest to the validity of this statement. The acts of discrimination, ethnic cleansing, racism, and the abuse of children, women, and men can never diminish so long as the victimization of ethical behavior remains in place for the sake of a desired end result. Whatever it takes to gain favor and prominence propels such conditions. Without the grounding effect that an education can provide regarding the value and effectiveness of substantive character, the outcome cannot be denied. The unintended consequence of disavowing his or her inherent credibility also remains in place.

The grounding effect is learning where the inherent credibility of an individual is realistically derived, and the commitment to put into practice this education. Such knowledge will help a person to resist the temptation to form deceptive dependencies on external and material sources for credibility. Without understanding the personal consequences to relying on external and material value for legitimacy, and using the accommodation and performance model for purposes of credibility, the unsuspected slowly becomes problematic.

This type of dependency, together with its model, is a formula for creating the opposite result from a desired effect.

The primary reason has to do with the individual having become a predisposed target for exploitation by both formats. Exploitation, because in a system of living that solely recognizes external and material successes as grounds for determining credibility, there is only one option available for a person to assess his or her personal value. Information regarding where and how the true value of an individual is defined is absent from the educational process. Religion speaks of such value, but keeps its icons at a great distance from its followers who are on record to having spoken concerning how that true value may be attained. Rather than focus on the works to replicate meritorious character, these individuals are idealized and elevated above the human realm.

Without such a process made readily available to expand the possibilities of achieving genuine credibility, an individual is limited to defining his or her personal value or the lack of value through experiences. As long as this pathway to legitimacy remains narrow in scope and kept afloat by the accommodation and performance model, the end result is foreseeable. A person walks away from his or her experiences feeling either worthy or unworthy, relevant or irrelevant, sanctioned or not sanctioned. Due to credibility being conditional within this format, such limited options for defining his or her value are in direct correlation to experiences that are either good or bad. Rather than live a life of stability based on inherent credibility as defined by the good traits of character, the opposite is made evident through the accommodation and performance model. This particular model is an impediment to living a life that exemplifies inherent relevancy, and where there is absolutely no need to prove his or her utilitarian usefulness.

The problems created within the accommodation and performance format exact a price. For one thing, an individual is expected to remain in perpetual motion proving his or her utilitarian potential with the hope of achieving what in actuality amounts to nothing more than conditional credibility. Though there is no guarantee of receiving the much-anticipated and -needed acceptance, proof of an individual's external and material value will take precedence over demonstrating the qualities of good character. The foremost priority within the accommodation and performance format is to heighten the value of utilitarian usefulness. Afterward, it is appropriate to then concern one's self with such issues of upright character. To fulfill the expectations of the accommodation and performance model necessitates taking full advantage of all the traditional methods used to provide a simulation of credibility and relevancy.

As it turns out, the more traveled pathway for achieving credibility is the tier-one version with its focus primarily on *what* an individual is externally. More traveled because a greater segment of humanity can achieve relevancy easier than through the tier two and three versions. The second variant places firm requirements regarding who is qualified to join such ranks of privilege. This will matter a great deal as the second tier of credibility reward an individual with a much-wider influence in terms of acquiring and exercising power, authority, and vision. Wall Street tycoons; CEO types; political and religious moguls; university presidents; high-profiled athletes; and motion picture, media, and music industry megastars fill the ranks of the second variant.

It is for this reason the traditional barriers used to impede credibility relative to the first tier, such as race, religion, ethnicity, age, and gender matter much less with the second and especially so with the third-tier variants of credibility. Relevancy and legitimacy for roughly 10 percent of the populace categorized as achieving tier-two credibility are principally associated with distinction of class, celebrity status, and credentialed education. It is economic prosperity that separates the second-tier type of credibility from the first tier. A concentration of wealth and dominance separates the third tier from the second and certainly from the first tier. Often referred to as the 1 percent, dominance and control of the world's wealth characterize this group's intention to establish relevancy based on global supremacy. In retrospect, all three tiers have a laser like focus on achieving credibility based solely on *what* a person is externally and possesses materially. Economic, social, religious, and educational inequalities and inequities are woven into the fabric of a system of living to help accelerate the process of individuals defining themselves by experiences.

Inequalities and inequities substantially assist the 1 percent, 10 percent, and the first tier to walk away from experiences defining themselves as relevant and credible due to external and material successes. Individuals outside the three tiers walk away from experiences defining themselves as unworthy and irrelevant due to not measuring up to the established external and material standards. Deficient in the knowledge regarding the value of one's intrinsic nature as this component of self pertains to the qualities of a comprehensive and good character guarantees a short-sighted personal definition. Lost is the opportunity to define oneself on a broader scale that exceeds the value of external and material measurements.

Lacking such understanding can cloud the following realization with seduction of self-interest. Self-importance and self-indulgence will necessarily push ethical boundaries beyond acceptable limits when the primary pursuit is consumed with personal gratification. Relying upon the accommodation and performance model to provide credibility will produce such results. The risk when taken can create a multitude of distress when going beyond ethical boundaries to achieve a desired satisfaction. Still, to attain even a pretense of credibility from unreliable external and material sources remains an attractive venture.

Referenced throughout previous writings is a proverb located in the Gnostic Gospels, Book of Thomas, and attributed to Jesus. It is of little significance, if any, whether Jesus is actually the author of the precept. What cannot be debated is the fact that the proverb was recorded for its message. The statement reads: "If you bring forth what is within you, what you bring forth will save you. If you do not bring forth what is within you, what you do not bring forth will destroy you." The ability to bring forth what will save a person from the irresistible temptation to yield submissively to self-importance and self-indulgence is nonexistent without an education regarding the intrinsic nature and value of good character. The means to establish personal value through the development of ethical and worthy personal qualities sidesteps the need to establish a sketchy reliance upon unreliable external and material sources. When self-importance and self-indulgence become the major internal influences for attaining legitimacy, forming a life based on credibility derived from genuine personal qualities becomes an unrealized opportunity.

Both influences inject misguided information and lead a person to undermine his or her best intentions. The inability to bring forth his or her inherent value as expressed through meritorious character can destroy an individual physically, spiritually, psychologically, and/ or emotionally. Due to strategies that lack substantive contributions from the intrinsic nature of character, a vital element of a person's humanity goes undernourished and underappreciated. Thus, heavily flawed by self-interest, and principally deficient in an ethical foundation, the best intentions pave a road for hell to begin taking root.

When relevancy is obsessively attached to power, authority, and the need to be right, self-importance and self-indulgence can act as an advanced guard for impoverishment to be outwardly exhibited. Its expression is customarily made evident through evil behavior. The more entrenched this internal condition, the more obvious is deception, duplicity, and corruption. Of course, the antidote for self-importance and self-indulgence will always be the character trait of humility. Self-absorption necessarily gives way to mutuality when the intrinsic nature and value of character is developed as a matter of course to bring forth what will save the individual.

When inequity and inequality become matter-of-fact components within a system of living that fails to rescind the growth of self-importance and self-indulgence with character development, the impact is all-inclusive. Regardless, both the injured and advantaged will rush to join the ranks commonly referred to as professional victims. In reaction to inequity and inequality, the injured will claim injustice, discrimination, and wrongdoing to legitimize rising complaints. And the advantaged will claim free market expression, the benefits of hard work, and reverse discrimination to justify success. Neither side of the equation realizes there is no victory when self-importance and self-indulgence are pitted against self-importance and self-indulgence.

The conversation taking place between the two sides will instantly disintegrate into a dual focused on who is right, and who can dismantle the credibility of the other most effectively. Once the focus turns to an issue of right, integrity and its properties of accountability, mutuality, and personal responsibility are sacrificed in favor of aggression, adversary, and retribution. Professional victims often establish loyalty to a distorted and sometimes perverted sense of self-importance and self-indulgence even if the ultimate cost is his or her life. The value of a human life beyond self-interest has never been understood nor established. But, this is what professional victims tend to do when the absence of the strength of character is apparent.

The inability to realize that each side of the discussion brings to the table valid points creates yet another lost moment to experience the essence of community. An indispensable occasion to experience a community of conscious living where it is possible to discover an agreed upon common good vanishes because of self-interest. In addition, within such a system of living where individuals define themselves by experiences, the injured and advantaged walk away from inequity and inequality with self-importance and self-indulgence in tow. The absence of an education to the strength of character perpetuates a historical condition of impoverishment that keeps both sides joined at the hip as professional victims. Both having lived down to one another's expectations, rather than living up to the worth esteemed through the honorable traits of character. Again, discovering where the good can take place will always be what a right measure to implement is, rather than finding ways to execute self-interest at the expense of that which is good.

Due to an insufficient training regarding a person's natural and complete growth process, which includes the development of traits comprising good character, the effect is to inherit a learning impairment. The impairment becomes entrenched when linked to an absence of encouragement from perceptive individuals who can recognize the deficiency. What helps to create a condition for the impairment to become embedded is the lack of inducement to pursue supplemental teachings with a focus on personal empowerment through character development. Thus, the void or limited information concerning the value of character leaves a person with only one option to utilize when it comes to defining him or herself. The lone option, which is to measure one's self as worthy or unworthy through personal experiences is solely relied upon to define his or her value. This is how and where the learning impairment exposes itself when relevancy or irrelevancy, significant or insignificant, adequate or inadequate are the only messages internalized from life experiences that are either good, bad, or indifferent.

The pathways to attain credibility are suitably designed with built-in conditions and restraints that accommodate the learning impairment. This design is to reinforce the condition of dependency in order to compensate for the lack of an education regarding the value of character development. Such an education would offset and offer balance to life experiences peaking as good, bad, or indifferent. When a person consciously or unconsciously permits himself or herself to be defined as worthy or unworthy based on experiences, impoverishment is the birth child. Again, this is the melting pot for the creation of self-importance and self-indulgence. Life minus an education regarding the intrinsic nature and value of character restricts a person's ability to choose and develop relationships outside the utilitarian model. In other words, a person is unable to recognize strength of character as a number one priority for any relationship when besieged with the message: "So what have you done for me lately?"

When inequalities and inequities are used to achieve credibility, while on the reverse side deny other individuals the opportunity to attain relevancy and legitimacy, enthusiasm is automatically chilled by a sobering dose of anxiety and insecurity. Whatever the gains, success must be rigidly preserved and protected against the threat of an infringement from sources that would attempt to nullify the initial infringement due to being excluded. When high-profile advantages are exposed that result from the unjust or prejudicial treatment of people or things on the grounds of class, economics, race, ethnicity, religion, gender, education, or age, the infringement is often brought to an end. Redress in one form or another eventually will occur, though it may take years, and in some instances, generations, to dismantle the damaging and harmful apparatus of oppression.

Reparations to the Native Americans, the end of American slavery, the right for women to vote, unemployment compensation, desegregation of the military and schools, child labor laws, voting rights act, and mortgage relief for refinance victims have been used to remedy the unjust treatment of people. Reducing the rate at which unjust and harmful infringements occur is a difficult endeavor. The combined economic and political influence representing privilege and entitlement effectively can take apart an effective countermeasure.

The distinguishable infraction may be rebuked, but a spin-off will often be created to achieve the same result as that of the initial infringement. Overt inequities and inequalities formed on the grounds of class, economics, race, ethnicity, religion, gender, education, or age discrimination can be blunted, but not eliminated. Such infringements return only to continue as a covert expression.

A system of living that elevates one group over another based on *what* a person is externally and possesses materially establishes an inbred process for a spin-off to materialize in a seamless manner. For the purpose of creating superior/inferior groupings, the process takes full advantage of the deficiency regarding an education to meritorious character. When an education regarding the intrinsic value and nature of character is made available, a coalition of equals will replace the need to build an empire. A concentration of power, authority, and relevancy in the hands of one or a few is a perfect setting for the infusion of abuse and corruption.

As stated before, because of a lack of education regarding character development, a person is left with one option when it comes to measuring his or her self-worth, or its lack. And that will necessarily be in relation to good, bad, and indifferent personal experiences. A boundary line comes into play to declare one side relevant and significant, and the other side irrelevant and insignificant. Even so, both sides of the line are based on manipulation and misrepresentation stemming from personal experiences. After years of legal proceedings, Affirmative Action was finally struck down as unconstitutional by America's highest-ranking judiciary, the Supreme Court.

Within the inner circles of privilege and entitlement, Affirmative Action was referred to as an infringement upon its rights. This coming from sectors of society that have benefited from economic, educational, and social disparities. It was believed that an allegiance to a quota system, rather than to the qualified, was just another form of discrimination. In point of fact, greater attention paid to a limited or fixed number of people was outright reverse discrimination. Affirmative Action was a strategical move to neutralize discrimination practices and feather into the workplace, housing, and especially upper learning institutions more balance concerning women and other minorities. Diversity was thought to advance learning and living experiences.

Once the defeat of Affirmative Action was complete, the effect was predictable. Firmly planted on each side of a border marked as a line of demarcation are self-importance and self-indulgence. The argument for right over good has afforded yet another opportunity to solidify the role of a professional victim with the one option in hand for measuring his or her self-worth or its lack. This, while holding steadfast with the superior/inferior groupings of humanity, and giving continence to "the more things change, the more they remain the same." As long as self-worth or its lack are measured by personal experiences, both sides of the superior/inferior equation will continue to isolate and remain in opposite corners from each other. Rather than define self-worth by the merits of character, which can unify due to a gathering of equals, isolation and fear dominate the line of demarcation. That is, until the next high-profile infringement takes place to bring both sides into the middle of the grievance arena.

The gist of yet another pointless skirmish will consist of who can outduel the other on the basis of being right. Let's not forget, professional victims are eager to stage an exposé to argue a point of view to justify his or her righteousness, which also provides a manufactured version of relevancy. Self-importance and self-indulgence are two sparks that continue to ignite the recurring clashes that take place between people who hold different perspectives regarding economic, racial, ethnic, gender, religious, or social inequalities and inequalities. The more people equate personal value with *what* an individual is externally and possesses materially, one urgent need is created to perpetuate the existing state of affairs. People are obligated to prolong

long-standing inequities and inequalities, as well as create new forms to substantiate living out the different perspectives.

Educate to the development and practice of worthy character and the different perspectives resultant from bias and discrimination will shrink. A major reason for the decline would be due to discovering other means to define his or her value other than through the narrow scope of personal experiences derived from inequities and inequalities: good, bad, or indifferent. Except when dreadful consequences are an outcome of practicing a distorted or perverted self-image, self-importance and self-indulgence are allowed to prolong their influences. On the daily menu are callous acts of self-serving privilege and entitlement which reveal abuse, greed, and deception as predominant means to attain or secure a base of power.

Without a personal invite from the interlopers and guardians of balance such as integrity, mutuality, and transparency, the repercussion is unsurprising. As can be expected, inequities and inequalities prevail as an acceptable succession of events shaped by self-importance and self-indulgence. Both are considered acidic potions that eventually erode the moral fabric of any human being's life. When the effort is made to educate to the value and practice of principled character, cohesion and adhesion will apply to more than just simple tribal connections.

The two conditions can reveal a morally conscious and responsive community having made the choice to accept a moral authority that is based on genuine credibility acquired through substantive character. Whereas, self-importance and self-indulgence are two qualities that consistently provide evidence of the impossibility to achieve cohesion and adhesion: tribal or otherwise. In addition, both furnish evidence representing a state of impoverishment, which has nothing to do with material or physical conditions.

It is important to grasp how the term "impoverishment" refers to an internal deficiency. The deficiency is due to an insufficient understanding and development of the intrinsic qualities that represent substantive character. An immediate reaction to overshadow this deficit is to develop commanding and self-confident attributes that, unfortunately, will morph into distorted versions of the genuine. Because the authoritative traits are manufactured, the degree of difficulty with the attempt to impersonate the authentic is extremely difficult to sustain on a long-term basis. Impoverishment seeks power first and foremost, especially over other individuals pursuing their value in the eyes of an external source. Authority that fundamentally lacks a commitment to practice mutuality, accountability, and personal responsibility eventually takes on dictatorship and autocratic characteristics.

Seeking from others what he or she refuses to give to others, and exerting an excessive amount of time saying what he or she does not mean are just two examples of autocratic attributes. The problem that never goes away for dictator-likes and autocrats is his or her inability to understand that "truth carries away what lies cannot counterfeit." The Achilles' heel for both the powerful and subservient is a truth that below the veneer of superior or inferior supposition is an element pertinent to humanity. And when this invaluable element of good resolve is allowed to develop, it will elevate personal credibility and value to establish an irrefutable gathering of equals: the merits of character. Even so, motivated solely by self-interest, the end game for the impoverished is the acquisition of power. Establishing personal value, which will always be a natural human instinct to fulfill, is mainly achieved through material and external gains. Factored into this equation are the societal inequalities and inequities that play a huge role in creating social imbalances.

Credibility and value outside the familiar are fair game for attack, especially since power and prestige are the standards of measurement for success. Thus, it matters not that an individual's public persona comes across as private, modest, active, animated or somewhere in the middle; self-importance and self-indulgence is laser focused on attaining power and stature. This manufactured authority will never replace genuine authority, where the intrinsic nature and value of character does not seek positions of superiority and prominence. Neither will genuine authority encourage nor accept a request to engage another individual or group that takes on a posture of superiority or inferiority. It is an act of futility to attempt any meaningful dialogue with self-importance and self-indulgence. The investment in being right and discrediting any different thought or suggestion can create a feeling of nausea or disgust. A person who adopts a position of superiority or inferiority will express points of view that expose a lack of understanding and education regarding how the true value of a person is derived.

The idea that a person's overall value as a human being can be measured by *who* he or she is inherently has received a wide range of opposition from every corner of the globe. The development and practice of a person's innate merits of character simply does not factor into the spoils of power, superiority, and prestige. The opposition to such a brazen idea is what strengthens the continued absence of any serious thought and effort to infuse into the educational format for humanity the intrinsic nature and value of good character. It is acceptable to call upon the words of past and present religious, civic, and philosophical icons who have spoken on the significance of educating to honorable character. The challenge of appealing on a conscious level to a humanity that is obsessive about consumption and immediate gratification has proven ineffectual.

For various social, economic, political, religious, and educational factions within the human landscape, the thought of building coalitions under ethical conditions is clearly out of the question. Keep the education, development, and practice of good character out of the minds of people, and one certainty maintains a constant presence. Self-importance and self-indulgence will continue as the number one crippler of the inability of the human race to advance beyond the misuse and abuse attributed to manufactured credibility. A human race lacking moral training and authority is left to its own demise and victimization, which, in a perverted sense, satisfies the misguided reasoning of the powerful and influential. To move beyond a protracted history of victimization and into a compelling account of human affairs finally provides relevance to credibility and quality of life. A dissimilar history, one that reveals the strength of character to be attributes such as accountability, transparency, and community would reduce the number of classic human burial grounds.

A scaling back of the number of graveyards filled to capacity with disappointed souls unable to detach from a learned infatuation with a false sense of security can be expected. Having achieved a balanced approach to attaining credibility and a consequential quality of life transforms the disappointed into a fulfilled life prior to running out of time. When character development becomes a necessary component of the educational process, the temptation to develop an affection associated with the deceitful appetite for false security quickly turns into a repulsive idea. This move to elevate the moral authority and standing of humanity will go a long way toward lessening in numbers a history of victimization. Well established inequalities and inequities continuously offered up as a feasible course to take in pursuit of credibility, which includes corresponding distorted interpretation of the quality of life will also arouse intense distaste or disgust. Income, employment, housing, education, health care, and other social imbalances become mute issues when character development becomes the centerpiece for individual and societal maturation.

It is not in any person's best interest to forget or ignore that the game is rigged, and it has been corrupted from the very start when *what* a person is externally carries greater value than *who* he or she is intrinsically. Whether achieved in a distorted or perverted manner, a system of living that values power and prominence over the education of character development also cultivates a rigged and corrupt way of life. No one should be surprised or horrified because abuse and misuse associated with inequities and inequalities are such an integral part of the human existence. In addition, a system of living that in principle and practice values above all else *what* a person is externally and *what* he or she possesses materially becomes the primary motivator to establish a built-in and heartless obsolescence. What matters today and is immaterial tomorrow is nothing to associate sustainability with: this is especially true when it comes to achieving and maintaining a manufactured form of credibility.

For the person who chooses to use inequalities and inequities for the purpose of attaining relevancy, it is important to know one indisputable certainty. Consistent with a way of life that considers the attributes of character to be insignificant makes available only one option for defining one's self. It is for this reason alone, why an individual is encouraged to learn the knowledge and his or her personal strengths made accessible through character development. To avoid the misfortune of defining one's self as worthy or unworthy, successful or unsuccessful based on experiences, extensive and far better results can be achieved through one vastly important discovery. The personal information and skills acquired from character development can provide a comprehensive definition of one's self embedded in the intrinsic nature and value of a person's character. It is a better road to travel down that will provide healthier options to define one's self when faced with age-old experiences stemming from inequities and inequalities that include either worthy or unworthy, relevant or irrelevant messages.

Even though inequalities and inequities may be used to gain an economic, racial, ethnic, gender, social, or religious advantage over another, one more indisputable certainty is set in motion. The experiences of success derived from unreliable and unethical strategies force the eventuality of unworthiness to make both a personal and cultural appearance. Again, a system of living that values the external and material while suppressing the virtue of character is always subject to what matters today will surely be rendered immaterial tomorrow.

To discredit one individual or group based on class, race, ethnic, gender, social, political, or religious differences, and yielding to an act of disrepute is to dishonor the virtue of all humanity, which would include one's self. Without fail, it is wise to remember that the individual or group who feels superior, dominant, inferior, and unworthy today can fall victim to the sharp blade of self-importance and self-indulgence as early as tomorrow. History is not shy nor bashful in revealing yet another indisputable certainty in this matter of balance. Though history is what it is, good and sound character continues to survive the coup attempts; it just needs to be taught more openly.

A way of life that boldly advocates for the practicality of credibility attributable to the merits of good character offers an individual the opportunity to find less and less attractive the unsustainable features of false security. The tenuous gains advanced through class, race, ethnic, gender, social, and religious inequalities simply are not worth the gamble of temporarily or permanently renouncing his or her individuality and soul. The absurdity of impersonating success or failure while ignoring the best a person has to offer his or her life, which are the merits of character, is finally realized when performing has run dry.

The exchange for attitudes that reveal superiority, privilege, inferiority, and irrelevance are all motivated by a personal state of impoverishment. It is an enterprise worth steering clear of altogether. In the long run, this game of chance is powerless to avoid the blade of self-importance and self-indulgence. Since integrity is a required component for cohesion and longevity to exist, it makes perfect sense with respect to the eventuality of a personal collapse. When allowed to transpire, impoverishment can easily be replaced with a relevance that self-importance and self-indulgence can never create nor call sustainable and reliable. Genuine credibility is the recognition of a birthplace where authentic legitimacy begins with an education to the nobility of character.

Chapter Seven

VULNERABILITY AND TRANSPARENCY

"When we were children,
we used to think that when we grew up we
would no longer be vulnerable.
But to grow up is to accept vulnerability,
to be alive is to be vulnerable."

Madeleine L'Engle

When it comes to the recognition of vulnerability and transparency as valid character traits, both have consistently represented a profound and puzzling dilemma for humanity to overcome. The acknowledgment as being valid on theoretical grounds has been quite easy. However, on a practical and applied basis, both traits are generally absent from personal usage. The responses to being vulnerable and transparent have always been two opposing and polarizing perspectives. One response has been to take the traditional viewpoint that reinforces a person to fear and reject both qualities. Such a perspective is completely opposite and in direct contrast to what Madeleine L'Engle says, "To be alive is to be vulnerable."

Optimum successes with relationships at home, work, and in social settings are directly related to the ability to demonstrate *who* he or she is regarding merits of character.

This, in combination with *what* he or she functions as and achieves, both externally and materially, will provide a balanced life. Success can be fragile and limited when this equation places a greater importance on *what* a person is externally and materially. To fear being vulnerable and transparent is to restrict the opportunity to experience honesty, authenticity, and success. There are no restraints or complicated approaches associated with success when *who* a person is regarding the innate gifts of character are included in the initiative to do the best in his or her life. Vulnerability and transparency are the two character traits that make certain this goal is accomplished through the gateway of authenticity.

Madeleine L'Engle's opening statement, "When we were children, we used to think that when we grew up we would no longer be vulnerable," captures a general consensus of never having to experience this trait as an adult. Ranging from youth throughout young adulthood, a common practice played out through relationships is the avoidance of being vulnerable or transparent. It simply is not in a person's best interest to exhibit either or both character traits. If he or she does not want to experience humiliation, rejection, or ridicule, it is wise to project a countenance of self-importance and self-indulgence. Of course, such reactions to vulnerability and transparency are inappropriate. However, the reactions are more than justified when living within a system that values power and superiority. Empowerment derived from character development is neither promoted nor valued when *what* a person is enjoys a sizable advantage in terms of worth.

Within this system of living, daily existence consists of attacking or fending off attempts to discredit or destroy in order for the aggressor to attain credibility and relevance. The higher up an individual is regarding personal status, the greater value he or she is given with respect to *what* that individual is externally and materially. With credibility and relevance being awarded for such value, vulnerability and transparency would certainly come under attack. And even in the absence of the two qualities, this system will still attempt to discredit and destroy any high-status individual. At the same time, the system rewards a person with prominence for his or her external and material achievements, impoverishment seeks to destroy the so-called hero. History is full of pages depicting the exploitation of people through the use of power by a dominant person or group in search of credibility and relevance. The customary reaction to vulnerability and transparency by the dominant force toward the weaker are frequently expressed in the form of outright abuse and oppression.

Bullying is a modern-day term used to describe the use of aggressive behavior, superior strength, or negative influence among school-aged children to intimidate smaller or weaker individuals. The nonaggressive and nonconformist tend to experience vicious attacks from primarily peers. These individuals are expressing a distorted use of power to achieve nothing more than a perverted sense of credibility and relevance. It is not uncommon for aggressive behavior to be directed at individuals who choose not to take on roles of power and superiority within a system of living that equates power with credibility. Vulnerability and transparency will consistently be a target of contempt. Impoverishment will resent any attempt to honor authenticity, while it remains a prisoner to a personal history of insincerity.

Bullying has always existed within a system of living that recognizes credibility to be based on an agenda that exclusively values external and material worth. This system elevates external and material worth to heights of distinction and status that are absurd. Ridiculous, because at the same time, this system totally ignores the value of two character traits responsible for unveiling the genuine: vulnerability and transparency. In fact, within such a value system, expressing areas of sensitivities through the attribute of vulnerability is viewed as a sign of weakness and areas to be exploited. A system of living that primarily bases credibility on manipulation and the acquisition of power to gain advantages over another person or group, vulnerability can be considered a means to achieve oppression. For this reason, it is not out of the realm of thinking to say that in youth and throughout young adulthood, an individual is taught to fear and feel intimidated by power. When there is a failure to educate to the merits of character, impoverishment can be convincing to use power to engage power, rather than truth speaking to power through vulnerability, transparency, and an authentic example of credibility.

At the beginning of Chapter 9 (Conclusion) are the prophetic words of the Native American elder, "Inside of me there are two dogs. One of the dogs is mean and evil. The other dog is good. The mean dog fights the good dog all the time." When asked which dog wins, he reflected for a moment and replied, "The one I feed the most." When there is a failure to educate an individual to his or her inherent gifts of character, the mean and evil dog will move into a position to overwhelm the good dog. The mean and evil dog will seize the opportunity through bullying or any other aggressive and cruel method to suppress vulnerability and transparency. This would include other legitimate qualities of sound character, as well.

The acts to control and repress vulnerability and transparency will first occur within that person who reacts with aggression, rejection, ridicule, and indifference toward others. Having been taught all too well through experiences to fear and feel intimidated by his or her own vulnerability and transparency, the consequence is clear. Having also accepted the idea that credibility and relevance are attained through power and domination, antagonistic and spiteful methods acted out against others is quite an acceptable behavior in reaction to vulnerability and transparency.

The mean and evil dog cannot allow to be displayed by others what he or she is fighting against internally not to surface. Compassion, originality, autonomy, mutuality, and innocence are met with condemnation and rebuff. The only exception would be to silence such reactions to one or more of these traits when pursuing a relationship based on accommodation and performance. The attempt to please and perform to expectations will be allowed to surface, because the conquest is extremely important. To test this theory, all a person has to do is look into a rearview mirror of the most recent and past histories. Throughout different regions of the world the collapse of corrupt governments and politics has occurred.

New leadership and politicians promise to usher in transparency to appease the accommodation and performance model. However, once the change has taken place, it is back to business as usual. The qualities of vulnerability, transparency, and accountability are moved to the background of human engagements. The history of revolutions reveals how every revolution in the end is the beginning of the next, because power and dominance are never dismantled in favor of empowerment. Class, race, ethnic, gender, age, and religious inequalities survive the purge.

For revolutions to reverse the tendency at its close and cease from being the beginning of the next, educating people to what is the best about him or her becomes a necessary step. Transparent throughout a new system of living equipped with this education will be the merits of character. Such an addition empowers the individual to achieve credibility and relevance without the assistance of inequities and inequalities. Moses, Jesus, the Prophet Muhammad, Gandhi, the Reverend Doctor Martin Luther King Jr., and Nelson Mandela were prominent leaders of celebrated human and civil rights movements.

The change that was brought about by these great leaders, unfortunately, did not bring lasting unification and consensus within their respective cultures. The focal points for the movements were the elimination of external oppression, but internal oppression within each culture was left undeterred. The major reason as to why oppressed groups, once having achieved a measure of success against repressive tactics, develop a way of life similar to the old system can be understood in a brief explanation. A historical precedent has been established on the part of both the leaders and their respective cultures that preserve old systems of living, as well as the old proverb, "The more things change, the more they remain the same."

The rebellions against oppression have mainly centered around the famed leadership of the notable civil and human rights movements. Though outward change occurred, the change that needed to take place within the various cultures under oppression never occurred. To avoid reestablishing a way of life absent age-old inequities and inequalities, the cultures would have been best served by devoting time to learning how genuine credibility and relevance are achieved. An educational program that explained the value and development regarding the inherent gifts of character would have disclosed how the two components of legitimacy are attained. This would have been an excellent foundation to build upon to provide a new system of living with different rules of engagement.

Replacing persecution, abuse, and tyranny with integrity, mutuality, and tolerance would have been a productive exchange to rid relationships of an intrusion of impoverishment. Instead, what materializes after a rebellion is the emergence of the mean and evil dog in the form of an internalized display of self-contempt. For example, Jew against Jew, Christian against Christian, Muslim against Muslim, Indian against Indian, African American against African American, South African against South African, and women against women. When a culture is embattled from within, the group becomes a target for oppression by outside forces.

Hence the statement, "united we stand, divided we fall" can come into play.

Another reason why oppressed groups develop a way of life similar to the old system of living has more to do with a limitation in terms of leadership skills. Upon having achieved a measure of success against an oppressive system of living, the tendency is for the masses to celebrate or worship great leaders of movements. Rather than build upon the wisdom, teachings and works of the leader with purpose to integrate empowerment on a personal basis, the leader is idolized or lionized. Movements fall apart and disappear or simply disintegrate into warring factions. Power regains its attractiveness, instead of relying on the credibility and relevance derived from character development where leadership skills are extracted. History has revealed one continuous reality upon the conclusion of a revolution. When the oppressed become the oppressor, power and domination have been kept alive from previous experiences with maltreatment. The end result is the extension of systems replicating inequities and inequalities that have been learned all too well.

The Christian faith has been the gatekeeper of a distinguished example that reveals how to initiate a new and distinct response when standing up in opposition to oppressive rule. This new system of living is based entirely on individual empowerment derived from the inherent gifts of character. Whether the revolutionary Jesus actually stated the prophetic words simply does not matter. The important point is the statement that can lead to personal freedom was brought to reality. As cited earlier, "And when he was demanded of the Pharisees, when the kingdom of God should come, he answered them and said, the kingdom of God cometh not with observation: neither shall they say, 'Lo here!' or 'lo there!' For behold, the kingdom of God is within you."[12]

---

[12] *Holy Bible (Authorized King James Version) Luke*: Chapter 17:20 21, "And when he [Jesus] was demanded of the Pharisees, when the kingdom of God should come, he answered them and said, the kingdom of God cometh not with observation: Neither shall they say, lo here! or, lo there! for, behold, the kingdom of God is within you."

Because Jesus has been idolized and lionized, it is difficult for humanity to emulate such a wise and profound method for achieving genuine credibility and relevance. In other words, Jesus has been made to be more than human, which means his wisdom and works remain beyond the reach of possibility for humans to mirror in their daily lives. Again, it is much easier to glorify Jesus, rather than to accept the personal challenge provided to humanity. To develop the inherent gifts of his or her merits of character, which exemplifies the kingdom of good would be the personal challenge Jesus left for humanity to gladly accept.

A system of living solely focused on attaining external and material value for credibility purposes will not hesitate to discredit and destroy a way of life with a different method to achieve legitimacy. This system will release its mean and evil dog any time vulnerability and transparency are articulated consistent with pursuing credibility outside external and material means. Quite the opposite is true with a system balanced with the recognition and value given to *who* an individual is in terms of his or her merits of character. The good dog comes alive to not only be in a position to adequately protect itself against destructive forces, but to substantiate the truth attached to L'Engle's statement, "to be alive is to be vulnerable." To express one's inherent gifts of character through the means of vulnerability is to be alive. To bring forth from within through the channel that authenticates and legitimizes life is the foundation for genuine credibility.

When individuals, communities, and nations commit to exemplifying leadership gifted with a passion and vision to elevate the whole person, rather than parts of the whole, one fact is a certainty. The character traits, vulnerability, and transparency will play a huge role. At the same time, humanity will legitimately stake a compelling claim to its own sanctity. By establishing credibility outside the margins of class, race, ethnicity, religion, politics, age, and gender, then the following characteristics of character, the very substance by which sanctity can exist, will have more meaning than mere rhetorical suggestions: Courage, original, strength, imaginative, resourceful, conviction, faith, confidence, sincere, passion, gratitude, loyal, civil, respect, vigilant, attentive, communicative, cautious, acknowledge, acceptance, kind, mutual, grace, responsive, appreciative, empathy, tolerance, sensitive, caring, congenial, contemplative, thoughtful, humility, community, reciprocal, generosity, compromise, encourage, nurture, inspire, forgiveness, consistent, continuity, fortitude, fair, authentic, cooperative, just, discipline, perseverance, steadfast, industrious, loving, adjust, ingenuity, creative, compassion, considerate, firm, apologetic, enthusiastic, conciliatory, genuine, accessible, patient, conserve, autonomy, congratulatory, approachable, hospitable, integrity, honest, reliable, trustworthy, dependable, dedication, accountable, inherent intelligence, recognition, commitment, introspective, vulnerability, transparency, and personally responsible.

Though many of the above attributes of character may indeed carry similar connotations to one another, the field is expanded intentionally to broaden and reveal the depth of character. When youth, young adults, and adults are educated to recognize, value, and live by the above-mentioned traits of meritorious character, social problems diminish in numbers. Crimes of passion, hatred, terrorism, suicide, poverty, homelessness, abortion, anorexia, bullying, alcoholism, drug addiction, bulimia, Ponzi schemes, mortgage fraud, abuse of children and adults significantly decrease. Educate to character and religious, civic, and political leaders can stop overpromising and under-delivering. Generally speaking, once leaders learn the value of being vulnerable and transparent with their agendas, the support for systems of living constructed on inequity and inequality quickly conclude.

Educational leaders can stop encouraging a practice that teaches a student how to be lazy, such as memorizing facts and dates for purposes of regurgitation. Instead, these same leaders can start encouraging the student to be vulnerable and transparent with his or her response to the question, "Tell me what you think?" Municipal leaders can stop encouraging division among their constituents. Time has arrived for the representatives of urban and rural strongholds to spearhead a concept of community. Exemplifying the type of vulnerability and transparency that can break new ground with social initiatives that identify viable pathways to unification can be a starting point. Religious institutions and leaders can, once and for all, stop being so heavenly minded where they are no earthly good. In other words, cease with complaining about what is not right in the world; cease with the use of superlative words and lofty statements when describing how people should be living their lives. To be any earthly good requires bringing heaven to this earth, not the blissfulness. Educate to character and there is no need to be heavenly minded; being authentic and genuine would be good enough.

To live life in a manner whereby vulnerability and transparency are the means that allow others to experience his or her gifts of character is the act of bringing heaven to this earth. It is truly a moment of transformation when this act at the same time inspires another to do the same or encourages him or her to begin a process of character development. It is foolish to harbor the thought that moral clarity, discipline, and fortitude can be brought about through legislative, political, or religious effort. Educate to character and humanity can make a compelling claim to understanding the sacredness of human life. Up to this point in its history, humankind has offered up a pleasing-to-the-ear rhetoric suggesting just how important the sanctity of human life is for purposes of moral clarity. However, until humankind recognizes that the most important and valuable component to human life are the inherent gifts of character that every individual is endowed with, then any claim to respect the sacredness of human life is simply unconvincing.

Digging a little deeper into this unconvincing claim for respect of the sanctity of human life, a powerful realization comes to the surface. What emerges are two harmful practices used by humanity that have proven, over time, to be an impediment to truly understanding the depth associated with the sacredness of human life. The practices are found to be a major component of a system of living that predominantly values *what* an individual is on an external and material basis. Within this system are two customs that overindulge or underindulge its youth and young adults through methods that basically reinforce deception and insincerity.

Unfortunately, both practices open the door for the youth and young adult to react toward authority and power with fear, intimidation, as well as with contempt. Also, it should be noted what additionally can be said about both practices is the inaccurate assessment regarding the character traits of vulnerability and transparency. As previously stated, the ill-fated estimation characterizes both traits as a personal liability. Both create an opportunity for others to gain a position of power, exert domination, as well as to reject on the basis of partiality. Rather than vulnerability and transparency being promoted as sources to help an individual access genuine qualities pertinent to his or her individuality, an opposite assessment is put forward.

In truth, this fear is real and justified. A system of living that establishes credibility and relevance solely based on external and material prominence will naturally create a "dog eat dog" culture.[13] People will do anything to be successful, even if what they do harms other people. Within the *what* you are culture, everyone fends for themselves. People compete with each other for success in a cruel and selfish way. If one can't take care of oneself, that individual will be eliminated. When a person is invested in receiving confirmation and recognition from external sources, while at the same time is expressing genuine qualities of character, the balance between the two

---

[13] "Dog–eat–dog Merriam-Webster," 2008. 4 Mar. 2016 http://www.merriamwebster. com/dictionary/dog%E2%80%93eat%E2%80%93dog

becomes problematic. Enthusiasm, faithfulness, and a team player might warrant receiving the gold watch from one hand after fifteen or twenty years of service, and the pink slip of termination from the other hand.

A system of living that tolerates a contradiction regarding the sanctity of human life will have no opportunity for the character trait of integrity to have real meaning. Theoretically, integrity will be worth some mention, but on a practical basis, it is nonexistent when self-importance and self-indulgence enter the conversation. The experience of rejection is difficult to manage when there is nothing in the personal portfolio for an individual to grasp upon with respect to his or her merits of character and the totality of existence. The ability to separate one's self from the experience of rejection by those in a position of power and authority is largely determined by one significant factor. Overall, the skill that is required to separate from experiences, especially rejection, is to know that credibility and relevance are actually based on the inherent merits of his or her character. To separate emotionally, psychologically, and intellectually from experiences that inflate or deflate his or her self-perception, this skill is absolutely important to personally develop.

The two customs of overindulging or underindulging youth and young adults through artificial means reveals a noteworthy revelation. Both customs through their respective practices deprive the individual of an opportunity to experience his or her innocence. When one-dimensional awards are given for recognition and importance devoid of an appreciation for the human element, innocence quickly evaporates. Limited credibility based on class, religious affiliation, race, ethnicity, and gender, as well as other forms of declared relevance that glorify *what* an individual is restricts self-perception. Rather than establish a multidimensional award system where *who* he or she is intrinsically also receives acknowledgment, credibility and relevance are gravely shortchanged. Since the primary focus is on compliance, accommodation, and performance, lost in the process is jubilation for integrity, humility, simplicity, and being good: all important properties of one's innocence.

The practice of overindulging youth and young adults has its serious repercussions in terms of living his or her life from a position of weakness or strength. The effect of inflating the importance of an individual undermines his or her capacity to personally appreciate and value the character traits of vulnerability and transparency. This deficit will have a person approaching his or her life from a position of weakness, but with education and appreciation, he or she approaches life from a position of strength. Power is always the display of a person living his or her life from weakness. Innocence coupled with vulnerability and transparency go hand-in-hand. The three qualities work together to radiate the genuine inner beauty of any individual.

That is, until these qualities are considered as unattractive and too risky for exposure. A system of living that is fundamentally constructed on external and material values will deter the unsuspecting from laying claim to a minority-held standard. The young person not yet comfortable with accepting his or her genuine value based on an innate credibility and relevance can be persuaded to reject what internally feels to be authentic. Culture and society can offer powerful incentives to help solidify the denial process. Class, race, ethnicity, gender, and religion will offer external credibility and relevance. Additional incentives to deny his or her inherent credibility will be the promise of relevance based on other *what* credentials . . . positions of authority regarding career, parenthood, physical beauty, and athletics, just to name a few attractive incentives.

For rejecting the incentives in favor of living his or her life based on an innate authority and credibility established through character development, the punishment is quite severe. The repercussions initiated by culture and society are rejection, ridicule, and isolation. So, the personal decision to avoid any repercussions is made and the philosophy "to go along, to get along" is easily adopted. Generally speaking, it will take a lifetime to personally discover that all the incentives offered to distract from accepting an authentic credibility and relevance failed to satisfy the internal desire to live one's life strictly based on his or her own life. The incentives have always been established to tempt him or her into living out a life that has nothing to do with the life of the person submitting to the seduction of external credibility and relevance. But, isn't that evil's intent, which is to discredit and to destroy?

This practice of overinflating the relevance of the youth and young adults communicates to the young person a dangerous message. The communiqué is that he or she is special merely due to *what* that person is relative to cultural and social credentials. Importance ascribed to the youth and young adult under these circumstances will play a major role in teaching the young person how to develop a distorted view of privilege and entitlement. Privilege not earned, but simply granted on the basis of *what* an individual is externally and materially, can put an end to innocence, vulnerability, and transparency. Consistent with this practice is the notion that it is appropriate to place in a position of responsibility someone or something, other than self, for a mistake or error in judgment. Emerging from this brand of education arises the basis for self-indulgence and self-importance, which is a destroyer of the person.

To establish relationships from a position of entitlement and privilege in conjunction with living as though he or she is beyond reproach cultivates a dangerous thought process. An inability to appreciate the significance of accountability for personal decisions and behavior are where the danger exists. An overinflated self-perception postured with a distorted privilege and entitlement, anchored by an absence of accountability, exposes an ethic inadequacy. Nonexistent is the principle of integrity, which is the cornerstone for sustainable success, and that includes relationships on all levels. Thus, vulnerability and transparency are phantom traits, as control, power, and deception become the skills used for personal interchange.

As a side note, adults directly or indirectly involved in the development of youth and young adults have a tendency to influence the process in a less-than-positive manner. For example, the technique of overindulging or inflating the importance of a young person places the adult in a posture of weakness and appeasement. The inability to say no at an early age when boundaries and limitations are needed to be established can turn into demands with rage attached at a later age. Rather than approach the young person from a position of strength and autonomy in the role of a parent, guide, or mentor, the adult seeks credibility and approval from the young person. The attempt on the part of the adult is to capture an experience that was lacking in his or her youth and young adulthood.

What was lacking during development for the adult was the recognition of his or her credibility and relevance based on genuine qualities of character from adult role models. Simply stated, during youth and young adulthood, mirroring and feedback identifying innate traits of good character comprising *who* the adult was did not take place. The experience that did occur during childhood and young adulthood were expectations of performance that the individual would fulfill for adult role models. Unfortunately, the expectations had nothing to do with the individual, but everything to do with the adult role models being reinforced as an authority figure in a position of power. "Do as I say, and do not question my judgment," is a common command often made by adult role models to children and young adults.

For the authority figure to feel relevant and in control, appeasement and accommodation on the part of the young person needs to occur to satisfy the adult's need to feel his or her sense of fulfillment. Credibility and relevance are granted on the basis of the young person's ability to satisfy the adult role model's expectation. Fast-forward to the young person in his or her adult life with efforts to champion and help his or her children, neighborhood youth and other young adults achieve success. *The Baby Boomers*—Boom Generation and Hippie subculture (1946–1964) and *Generation X*—Baby Busters (1965–1980) tend to respond to youth and young adults as their adult predecessors; as strict disciplinarians. For example, parents can often be observed exerting out-of-control anger and frustration at the ballgames, skating rinks, music and dance lessons. This behavior is usually in reaction to mistakes made by the child, young adult, or officials in-charge of overseeing the activities. However, *Generation X*—MTV Generation and Boomerang Generation (1975–1985), *Generation Y*—Millennials, Echo Boomers, or Generation Why? (1978–1990), and *Generation Z*—New Silent Generation (1995–2007)[14] tend to respond with a more tolerant and sensitive approach toward the child or young person. There are instances when over-indulgence can be problematic for these generations. There is a tendency to neglect holding the child or young person accountable for lessons to be learned from mistakes.

Rather than be a successful parent, guide, or mentor, many adults have instead chosen to be a friend or confidant to the young person. Rather than approach the young person from a position of autonomy and independence in the role of a parent, guide, or mentor, the youth and young adult are elevated to a status equivalent to that of the adult before it is appropriate. As previously stated, the pressing danger is that the lines of autonomy between parent and child become reversed and extremely blurred. Moreover, if a parent is so willing to elevate his or her child to a status of privilege in order for that parent to gain some measure of credibility, then this becomes an expectation the child will take into his or her adult life, not to

---

[14] Isacosta' Site, List of Generations Chart http://www.esds1.pt/site/images/stories/isacosta/secondary_pages/10%C2%BA_block1/ Generations%20Chart.pdf.

mention an underlying contempt for the parent who is dependent on the child for self-assurance. What's more, future relationships that the child establishes will be based on his or her distorted sense of personal privilege and entitlement.

Again, this is an example of how a young person's innocence, along with the inherent attributes of vulnerability and transparency, are systematically undermined and taken away. An afterword to this practice is how difficult it is for some adults to allow the youth and young adult to have the opportunity to experience his or her innocence, vulnerability, and transparency. Difficult, indeed, when such experiences were not made available by adult role models during their youth and young adulthood. Nevertheless, this is how contempt toward authority and power is developed on the part of the youth and young adult. Elevated to a position of privilege and entitlement before learning the skills of discipline, sacrifice, and personal responsibility, there simply is no room for respect of authority when that same authority has the need to elevate the young person to that level of their so-called superior.

Rather than educate a person to recognize and value his or her inherent gifts of character, credibility is instead attached to a skill set based on accommodation and performance. Innate gifts of character, such as mutuality, integrity, generosity, vulnerability, originality, and civility are simply ignored during an individual developmental process. How well a person can satisfy the needs of another through the exploits of accommodation and performance is the basis that determines credibility and relevance.

Instead of encouraging a person to experience his or her qualities of meritorious character through distinctive individuality, questioning that is respectful, and cultivating critical thinking, the opposite is taught. Individuality is downplayed in favor of going along to get along. Questioning is not encouraged for fear of reprisal, and critical thinking gives way to memorizing and regurgitating data to establish the appearance of credibility. Personal wholeness and completeness is interpreted as being equivalent to how much external and material confirmation and validation a person can achieve during his or her lifetime.

Underindulging or deflating the quality of being worthy of importance with respect to the youth and young adult also has its serious consequences. The practice undermines his or her ability to personally develop an appreciation for the character traits of vulnerability and transparency. In fact, vulnerability and transparency will oftentimes be viewed as a trait representing a person who is emotionally and physically weak. In addition to this judgment, the person can also be viewed as an easy target for abuse or misuse. It should be noted that the inability to develop an appreciation for attributes of good character as an adult is, again, a consequence of early developmental experiences. Being exposed to the practice of underindulging or deflating the relevance of a youth and young adult paves the way for that individual to cheapen the attributes of good character as an adult.

Absolute rulers, dictators, authoritarians, and tyrants totally believe in underindulging or deflating individuals for the sole purpose of exerting and maintaining power over a captive audience. As with the practice of overindulging, where the youth and young adult are taught to assume a posture of privilege and entitlement, the opposite is true with underindulging. Overindulging a young person takes place when adults in positions of authority choose to take on positions of weakness and appeasement to achieve credibility. Whereas, underindulging takes place when adults in positions of authority choose to exercise power and domination to achieve credibility at the expense of the young person. As with the practice of overindulging, the same accommodation and performance is expected from the young person under the conditions of overindulging.

However, there is one significant difference between the practice of underindulging and overindulging. With underindulging, repercussions for not satisfying the expectations of adult role models tend to be greater and more severe for the young person. Families, communities, cultures, and religions can be ruthless with retaliation against a person who dares to marry outside of his or her ethnicity, religion, race, or class. Ex-communication, ostracism, removal from the family will, and even the loss of life can be repercussions for not following the wishes of an authoritarian rule. Especially within the underindulging way of life, the young person has two principal duties. The first duty is to inflate the credibility and relevance of individuals wielding the power through compliance and conformity, which equates into obedience. The second principle duty of the youth and young adult is to deflate his or her credibility and relevance through subjugation that leaves evidence of gratitude.

Consistent throughout the practice of underindulging and deflating, the young person has no voice and is invisible to his or her environment. Even with a restricted credibility, the adult authoritarian must have his or her self-importance and self-indulgence protected at all times, or the limited relevance is further regulated. Again, this a favorite position to take for rulers who have absolute power representing families, ethnic and racial groups, political, educational, work, and religious organizations. Because power and domination are the basis by which adults establish relationships with the youth and young adult, privilege and entitlement are also established by the adult in a position of authority.

The foundation, which has always been the chief support for the creation of inequalities and inequities, plays a major role in maintaining this system of living. "To seek from one another what we refuse to give to one another," remains a linchpin that keeps the wheel of oppression rolling along generation after generation. As the youth and young adult are mandated to follow and remain voiceless, is there any wonder why Madeleine L'Engle's statement reverberates so profoundly for the youth and young and young adult? "When we were children, we used to think that when we grew up we would no longer be vulnerable."

The overindulged and under-indulged are victimized by holding onto a misguided faith to a system of living fixated on recognizing as credible the value of *what* an individual is externally and materially. This misguided faith linked to achieving personal redemption through external means also extends to include a misguided belief. The notion that a commitment to attaining credibility and relevance in this fashion will insulate that person from the consequence of ignoring the value of character development is ludicrous. Cultivated by a distorted perception of self-importance and driven to accumulate power and notoriety by burying one's self inside an external and material lifestyle calls into question personal soundness. Absent the principle of integrity, and where hope and protection are to be more than plentiful to offset this transgression is delusional. Having been prepped by either the overindulged or under-indulged practice to develop a skill set of power in place of character development, personal and moral growth is shortchanged.

Attributes such as vulnerability and transparency, two traits that help to develop emotional and spiritual maturity, are cast aside. As a consequence, for this deficiency, an internal condition of immaturity and impoverishment develop, no matter how well he or she is held together externally and materially. Educate to character and humankind will cease to seek from one another what it refuses to give to one another. It becomes an intuitive inclination to help one another to become the best that he or she can be, and not because it is the right thing to do. It simply is a good deed to achieve, because the act brings forth from within *who* that individual is in terms of character. This is a sure way to elevate and advance life, both for the provider of goodwill and the recipient. In addition, the character traits, vulnerability and transparency, are two compelling qualities that will discourage an individual from falling under the spell of self-betrayal. Contentment with one's self and his or her place in this world is an inside job, not contingent on an external mirage or oasis appearing on the doorstep.

The reward for being true to one's self is a stand-alone credibility and relevance that can produce too much personal satisfaction to jeopardize. It is truly unfortunate the powerful view both traits as signs of weakness, which only guarantees their internal state of impoverishment. It is truly fortunate the empowered view both traits as a gateway to personal freedom. Developing a collection of internal assets that represent an admirable character will not win any rewards, nor will there be bells and whistles. What he or she receives for the work is just a contented soul at ease with the ability to add an example for humanity to experience that amplifies substantive credibility and relevance.

Again, vulnerability and transparency that fearlessly reveal the effectiveness of sound character are two attributes that will deny any potentiality of internal impoverishment and self-betrayal. Both will elevate the personal journey for credibility and relevance, while at the same time, give honor to the sanctity of human life. Regardless how one may dress it up or down, without moral clarity, discipline, and fortitude, personal stability is a ghost of an idea. And without the merits of character, impoverishment guarantees the instability of any person attempting to make a ghost out of an idea lacking qualities that are distinctively good and substantive. Internalized disappointment for feeling deficient because he or she was unable to reach or stay perched atop the pinnacle of external recognition in due course reaches a point of no return. Vulnerability and transparency, coupled with recognition, value, and a commitment to demonstrate *who* an individual is, accomplishes a major personal goal. In terms of his or her merits of character employed as a personal vanguard, the door is shut to intrusive thoughts that would suggest seeking credibility and relevance from sources here today and gone tomorrow.

In closing, it bears repeating that the pathway to establishing personal credibility that is enduring and meaningful will consistently be through the recognition and demonstration of the merits of an individual's character. The validity and originality of one's voice will be recognized and strengthened, as well. More importantly, a person has the opportunity to define him or herself by more information that is genuine than just experiences. It is not enough to memorize and recite chapter, verse, page, amendment, and founding documents that represent the wisdom and voices from important historical figures.

Developing his or her individuality to establish an authentic voice and personal wisdom is a more meaningful path to pursue. When there exists the inability to develop merits of sound character, there also exists the inability to develop a personal voice expressing wisdom that can help to elevate humanity, as a whole. Memorization and recitations are meager intellectual exercises that lack personal conviction. Such methods of learning are designed to maintain a status quo of power and deception for those individuals interested in building empires.

When an individual is lacking the education and value regarding good character, it is difficult for that person to believe he or she can be credible and relevant on a genuine level. Self-perception is one that lacks personal depth and meaning. This is why external achievements resulting in external recognition provide some form of relevance: be it conditional. Moral clarity, discipline, and fortitude simply are out of this person's emotional, intellectual, and spiritual reach. The lesson to be learned is that no nation, ethnicity, religion, or political party has a monopoly or can dominate the flow of knowledge and wisdom. Both can pertain to a pathway that establishes personal credibility based on *who* an individual is in terms of good character.

Self-perception gains depth as his or her inherent credibility and authority are transitioned through the knowledge and wisdom that represents individuality full with the gifts of character. Educate to the merits of character and his or her inherent credibility will be represented by a voice of authority that is both inclusive and innately good. And the means to help with this expression will reliably be the character traits of vulnerability and transparency.

The notable American Jungian analyst and author Robert A. Johnson comments on individuality in his book, *Inner Work*: "Individuality or individuation is the process of waking up to our total selves, allowing our conscious personalities to develop until they include all the basic elements that are inherent in each of us at the preconscious level."[15] Educate to the merits of character and this basic inherent element awakens the student to an understanding regarding his or her authentic credibility and relevance.

---

[15] Robert A. Johnson, *Inner Work*, HarperCollins Publishers, 10 East 53rd Street, New York, NY 10022 (page 11).

Chapter Eight

THE ISSUE OF IMPOVERISHMENT

"Happy is your grace that can translate the stubbornness of fortune into so quiet and so sweet a style."

William Shakespeare English Playwright, Poet, Actor

In order to understand concepts set forth in this chapter, it is necessary to briefly return to the previous chapter regarding the subject of vulnerability and transparency. It is common knowledge to the individual seeking to be authoritative and dominant, the character traits, vulnerability and transparency, are perceived as signs of weakness. This point of view can be expected to be a personal belief when he or she is in support of a system of living that attaches relevance to prominence and power. Consistent within this system that cultivates deception are the interpersonal interactions that mainly focus on destroying the credibility of another person or group. Distorted is the motivation, for the initiator attempts to achieve credibility and relevance for him or herself through negative behavior.

The daily attempts to discredit and destroy with this purpose in mind can be easily observed under the headings of international and domestic terrorism, military, social issues, politics, race, ethnicity, religion, economics, gender, sports, and the workplace. For the person who persists in pursuing recognition from this externally focused value system, while naïvely using the innate attributes of vulnerability and transparency, the lack of relevance could prove disastrous. The attempt to remain loyal to a system of living that cares very little, if any, about genuine relevance makes a person an easy target to be discredited—and even destroyed at any moment. Considering how credibility is closely associated with superiority and power regarding *what* an individual is externally and possesses materially, it is wise to know the following. The sanctity of human life is related to external credentials, rather than to the inherent nobility of the individual— the gifts of character.

On the contrary, the person educated to his or her merits of character, vulnerability, and transparency are viewed as the gateway to empowerment and authenticity. Depending on which side of the character development argument a person is positioned, the response to choosing vulnerability as a personal attribute has always been a choice between weakness and strength. To perceive vulnerability as a weakness is to side with the traditional practice of resisting and rejecting the attribute of transparency, as well. Nonetheless, vulnerability is a practical and effective attribute that can reveal the best components of a person's individuality. And with the development of his or her merits of character to protect personal distinction, relevance and credibility are never in doubt of losing legitimacy.

Those who reject this idea do so because of a commitment to support a value system that places enormous importance on establishing credibility through external and material means. *Who* an individual is intrinsically in terms of substantive character has very little relevance within this way of life. Vulnerability does not have a credible place within a way of life dominated by external value. Instead, the acquisition of power and supremacy over another person or group are the end game for individuals that embrace this particular way of life. Vulnerability and transparency are strictly viewed as a hindrance, not as an asset.

The reverse is true for individuals who embrace and have an appreciation for authenticity, integrity, and complexity. Character traits, such as vulnerability and transparency, are considered windows of opportunities to experience a credibility and relevance undeterred by the "fickle finger of fate." An education to the merits of character is what makes it possible for a person to develop an appreciation for a personal relevance that cannot be discredited or destroyed by external uncertainties. In addition, meaningful relationships with a focus on maximizing attributes of individuality will heavily invest to protect its relevance.

And the best investment would be to recognize the credibility of intrinsic value as it pertains to *who* each person is in conjunction with demonstrating the attributes of good character. Again, to reach this level of conscious thinking, the education regarding the value and effectiveness of good character and its development is a necessary prerequisite. Without this education, an internal vacuum is created, rather than attributes of sound character. Because character development is absent, this deficiency can have lasting implications throughout a person's life. The absence warrants this condition to be described as a state of impoverishment.

This lasting implication, referred to in the previous paragraph, can best be described as an individual's inability to separate self-perception from personal experiences. Good experiences are used to define one's self as relevant, credible, and worthy. Bad or indifferent experiences are used to define one's self as irrelevant, lacking, and unworthy. There is little to no information available outside of personal experiences that properly educates an individual to know that he or she is defined by more than just experiences. For this reason, discrimination and injustice play a major role in providing experiences on both sides of the negative and positive spectrums that help shape self-perceptions.

Class, social, racial, ethnic, religious, age, and gender inequities and inequalities have been a landscape mainstay from the beginning of humankind's existence. And the same injustice and discrimination practices will continue to exist for systems of living that educate to the type of relevance that values power and prominence over empowerment. To maintain an imbalanced system of living strictly based on the influence of external factors to determine credibility is to invite deception and corruption to become contributors to the creation of relationships. Casting aside a more balanced system influenced by an inherent value linked to meritorious character sets the stage for a greater intrusion—referred to as impoverishment.

Who a person is as confirmed by the existence of intrinsic value, and preserved by the development of his or her merits of character, should be of equal relevance to *what* a person is externally and possesses materially. Neither should be opposed to the other when both are distinguished by one's merits of character. To avoid the gravity of inequities and inequalities and the pull into self-betrayal through deception and corruption, it helps to know the attributes of principled character to protect individuality. The exploration and development of individuality expands the self-perception an individual brings to the pursuit of credibility and relevance when based on the merits of character development. However, if a lack of knowledge and value regarding the personal attributes of good character start to take root, so does the state of impoverishment. As previously stated, this deficiency and vacuum eventually fills with worthy or unworthy self-perceptions dependent on experiences. Impoverishment can certainly exist and flourish in the midst of material affluence. There is nothing to counteract the perceptions, such as expanded conscious thinking reflective of character development.

Robert A. Johnson, author of the book *Inner Work*, states:

> In modern Western Society, we have reached the point at which we try to get by without acknowledging the inner life at all. We act as though there were no unconscious, no realm of the soul, as though we could live full lives by fixating ourselves completely on the external material world. We try to deal with all the issues of life by external means: making more money, starting a love affair, or accomplishing something in the material world. But we discover to our surprise that the inner world is a reality that we ultimately have to face. If we try to ignore the inner world, as most of us do, the unconscious will find its way into our lives through pathology, psychosomatic systems, compulsions, depressions, and neuroses.[16]

The impact from this impoverishment can be tracked when feelings that occur in the moment of an experience are not responding to being filtered on a conscious level. Instead, due to an accumulation of experiences resulting in the same or similar negative conclusions that remain personally unresolved, the feelings hardened into emotions. The hardened feelings can combine with previous calcified feelings stemming from identical or similar experiences. As a general rule, feelings have a relatively short life span, while emotions have a longer life span, depending on whether resolution has occurred. Without a background of character development, experiences that can act as a provocation for feelings to calcify into emotions are abuse,

---

[16] Robert A. Johnson, *Inner Work*, HarperCollins Publishers, 10 East 53rd Street, New York, NY 10022 (page 10).

abandonment, failure, disappointment, rejection, and loneliness. A person who has a personal history of being physically or sexually abused and lacks sufficient recovery that resolves the rage, anger, and victimization can become an angry man or woman prone to reenact the abuse. Essentially fueled by calcified emotions, victimization of another innocent soul becomes the foremost objective.

A person who experiences lengthy periods of feeling unloved and lonely can yearn for attention to a point that he or she will engage in relationships that provide an even greater degree of discredit and loneliness. This self-perception is most likely to emerge when a person is absent an education to the merits of his or her character. Value and appreciation for the personal traits comprising *who* an individual is inherently rule out participating in relationships that consider accommodation a viable reason to come together.

Better to be alone with dignity than to be routinely reminded of conditional acceptance to ward off loneliness and the fear of being ruled irrelevant. To have relationships that showcase authenticity and individuality, rather than racing to satisfy cultural demands for beauty, opulence, and prominence, makes it much easier to sleep at night. Being alone is vastly different from loneliness, which translates into an absence from oneself. Educate to the value and practice of the merits of character and attributes such as vulnerability, transparency, and accountability need not create fear and shame, but joy and personal empowerment.

Another example for how calcified emotions may appear would be feeling like a failure and unworthy after being permanently laid off from work due to cost-saving measures. Similar emotional reactions from past experiences that were internalized as being rejected could come alive in the memory bank to link with the job loss. A spouse or partner who decides to leave the marriage or relationship due to falling out of love and a lack of interest could reinforce a person's internalized sense of unworthiness and failure. Again, the absence of an education to the merits of his or her character makes it very difficult for a person to separate himself from feelings of unworthiness and failure.

This is largely true when feelings have hardened into emotions over a period of time due to a gradual gathering of experiences of never measuring up to external values. Alcoholism and drug addiction, obesity, anorexia, or bulimia helps to augment an internalized self-perception of being a failure. The individual can remain on a track to repeat destructive behavior or until such time he or she learns to define oneself by more than just experiences. It's a vicious cycle that keeps this person trapped inside a system of living that offers nothing in the form of character development. There is nothing to offset negative experiences with a more complete and truthful manner to define him or herself.

The same challenges exist for individuals and groups who have attained power and prominence strictly due to *what* he or she is externally and possesses materially that results in an elevated credibility and relevance. The effort not to define oneself and separate his or her credibility and relevance from external factors is an extremely difficult task to undertake. This is especially true when such external elements produce the type of success that elevates the person or group above other people. Wall Street and business executives, politicians, religious leaders, athletes, and high-profile celebrities often have trouble not attaching personal worthiness to their positions in life. As expected, race, ethnicity, religion, educational credentials, gender, and age are also means used to elevate credibility and relevance to achieve power and prominence.

The birth of inequalities and inequities has come about for no other purpose than as a way to achieve and preserve positions of power and prominence. With an obsession to experience relevance at any cost, steroids, drugs, alcohol, corruption, and other white/ blue-collar crimes become unavoidable experiences associated with

attaining and maintaining prominence. This fabricated form of credibility and relevance achieved solely through external means has
come to be attached to entitlement and privilege. A person gets to say
and do whatever he or she feels without any thought of consequence
or injury to another person or group. Destroying the credibility of
another person or group or simply destroying the person or group
are not out of the realm of possibilities in order to hold onto power,
control, or prominence. It is especially difficult to reduce evil and its
effect, while practicing various degrees of wickedness.

Again, this is a good example of impoverishment. Deficient in the
personal development with respect to his or her merits of character
limits a person from grasping a wider scope regarding the distinction
of personage. Without question, external accomplishments are a
splendid way to experience passion and conviction wrapped around
talent. However, with a deficiency in character development, external exploits motivated by "the end justifies the means" become the
only manner to experience credibility and relevance. If the person
is resistant to taking responsibility to reverse this internal condition
of impoverishment through character development, the outcome is
predictable.

To learn how genuine credibility and relevance are derived versus
learning methods to accommodate a conditional form of importance
avoids investing in a life equivalent to a house of cards. Because
personal responsibility is not an attribute thought to have credibility
within a system of living mainly external and material value, the
deficiency has harmful results. Reasons and causes that deflect from
the real problem become the responses when destructive privilege
and entitlement impacts the life of another individual or group. To
seek release from guilt, obligation, or punishment, the effect of impoverishment will often be displayed through attempts to blame and
discredit the victim. Look no further to witness the misuse of power

and entitlement through acts of domestic violence, police brutality, and the collapse of economic systems.

The development of sound character produces one certainty that will not be contingent on the inconsistency and duplicity of external factors. The foundation of an individual's genuine credibility and relevance will have nothing to do with *what* he or she is in terms of job, profession, or credentials. To the contrary, the foundation will have everything to do with *who* an individual is regarding the inherent nobility attached to his or her distinctive individuality. One attribute that draws a great deal of importance as a result of the development of sound character is integrity, which is the cornerstone for credibility and relevance. The impoverished strongly resist accepting this assertion, as can be witnessed during an incident in which injustice is being addressed.

Without the attributes of character to intercede, the impoverished remain firmly committed to the belief that the lack of integrity will heal or bring to justice the lack of integrity. Revenge acted out through violence in response to injustice cannot heal the lack of integrity. Such actions only create the often repeated scenario, "the more things change, the more they remain the same." Disgrace and dishonor are the consequences of having no regard for the sacredness of human life, because moral clarity, discipline, and fortitude cannot be produced when the best part of an individual is under siege by a bloated body or ego. Therefore, the education and value attributed to sound character and its development is a need that is never wanted.

When committed to pursuing credibility within a system of living that encourages a person to focus his or her efforts on satisfying external criteria, negative consequences emerge. With respect to personal responsibility, legitimate needs, such as to love, to be loved, cared for, appreciated, and to be heard are delegated to outside resources for purposes of accommodation and validation. Under such conditions he or she is expected to adapt and adjust to resources that will leverage various degrees of power over the individual. For instance, within many cultures, it is expected that a person date and marry within his or her own race, ethnicity, religion, class, and political ideology. If the expectations are not satisfied, condemnation and rejection within the inner circle by persons yielding power are most likely to occur.

Condemnation and rejection by a mother and/or father, family, community, and church can create internal messaging on the part of the rejected. The messaging can often be internalized that he or she is a disappointment, disgrace, and failure for not satisfying the expectations of the authoritarians. When the development of good character has taken place, seeking credibility through external sources for purposes of approval and validation is nonexistent. Genuine needs responsibly fulfilled will represent a credibility and relevance primarily derived from resources within an individual who understands his or her true value. Internal applause will always be heard when taking personal responsibility to satisfy legitimate needs—with integrity leading the way throughout the process.

The proverb, "Personally become what it is that you want; become what it is that you need," places the responsibility for bringing into one's life wants and needs squarely on the shoulders of the individual. As the overused cliché goes, "If it is a friend that a person desires, then he or she has to first learn how to be a friend." Learning how to be a friend first to one's self sets the stage to be a friend to another person. If it is to feel loved, seen, heard, and appreciated that one desires, then he or she is responsible to first learn how to develop and love the best qualities that comprise one's character. Such a personal journey will also reveal *who* he or she is intrinsically.

In addition to this discovery, an individual will be able to experience other people from the vantage point of *who* they are inherently. Becoming skilled at listening and learning to appreciate without preconditions develops meaningful relationships. If this discovery is not made through the process of recognizing the effectiveness and value regarding the merits of one's character, then the following comes to fruition. It becomes extremely difficult to make sensible decisions and to exercise prudent judgment regarding relationships and career choices.

The impoverished persistently wait for something or someone else to become that which they want or desire. Again, this is a formula for establishing unholy alliances. This is a major reason why dating, courtship, and romantic relationships formed inside the bar and tavern often turn out to be disastrous experiences. The game afoot is to transform one's self into what each participant perceives the other wants to see and hear. Furthermore, the misunderstanding that a person should attempt to attain from another individual or material object what he or she is already in possession of internally speaking is more evidence regarding impoverishment.

It's just that the individual has never been educated to look within to understand that the merits of his or her character provide the greatest form of credibility, stability, and resourcefulness. When the focus is primarily directed at achieving credibility mainly from external and material sources, instead of using the attributes of good character—personal disgrace and dishonor can be the end result. Abuse of credit, loss of jobs, chronic unemployment, bankruptcy, home foreclosure, loss of retirement savings, repossession, hostile divorce, and suicide can be consequences linked with the drive to pursue external and material resources to achieve credibility and relevance.

An unspoken, but distinct internal cry that can be clearly heard from any individual who attaches him or herself to a system of living that mainly recognizes external and material value is "prove me worthy." It is an internal cry that can escalate to a feverish pitch as an individual commits more and more time and energy to this system of living. Because the responsibility for achieving personal worth and credibility is extended outward, rather than inward, it becomes imperative to find that individual as well as tradition, such as marriage, bearing children, career, religion, and politics that will establish the individual's credibility.

Imperative, because no individual wants to feel he or she lacks credibility or relevance; the two are natural human instincts. A person will often choose inappropriate partners and friends, enter into inappropriate relationships, and ultimately engage in behavior that undermines his or her personal dignity.

Again, the stage is set for unholy alliances to emerge, which initially are established to prove credibility and relevance. The struggle for dominance, influence, and independence can be quite intense, which can leave long-lasting internal scars. The choice of partners and friends is not about who, but what an individual represents on an external and material basis. Under such circumstances, the unintended consequences continue to be spelled out in terms of disgrace, dishonor, and embarrassment. The drive to be proven relevant through relationships, interaction with others, and traditions are established on the ability to effectively accommodate and satisfy the "prove me worthy" agenda.

The attempt to discredit anyone or any ideology that is not in line with this agenda will consume a great deal of time and effort. A system of living based strictly on external and material values encourages its populace to fragment around power, rather than to coalesce around empowerment. Nonetheless, there is a backside to such consequences, no matter how painful and unsettling. The unplanned consequences do provide opportunities to learn valuable lessons that can teach the difference between what is genuine and what is imitation: that is, if the individual is open to self-examination. However, if there is no openness to self-examination, then legitimate and sustainable credibility will continue to be an elusive experience, and the condition of impoverishment will remain intact.

It is not uncommon to be annoyed with feeling empty and ineffective when lacking an education as to the merits, strength, and value of character. In order to bring balance to personal development, it is imperative to experience this education. The self-perception of not being enough externally or having enough materially will be a constant companion without the development of sound character. It makes for perfect logic that there would then be the need to create a superficial credibility based on class, race, ethnicity, religion, gender, and political distinctions. It also makes for perfect logic that a personal obsession would be created with using work, sex, money, physical beauty, fashion, marriage, childbearing, and the acquisition of power to fill the empty and void cavities.

The modus operandi is simply to use anything and everything to distract from those internal cavities. A self-perception of being a person that is deficient and lacking is clearly not permissible. This is especially true when living in a nation, family, and community with wealth and prosperity. When personal meaning, purpose, and most of all, credibility, are primarily sought through external and material means, one given fact is a certainty. External stimuli are needed to satisfy the internal longing to feel good enough and sufficient. Rather than seek personal meaning through the recognition, demonstration, and value given to the merits of character, the external achieves one goal—enough is never enough.

This is not a new idea. There have always been two systems of living from which humanity can choose. Both need the quality of vulnerability to be fully in play as a sign of commitment, but for very different purposes. Both systems reward an individual for his or her loyalty, enthusiasm, and vulnerability in dissimilar ways. In a system of living that supports the sanctity of human life through the development of an individual's inherent gifts of character, there is no in-house beast bellowing out distressing internal feelings of emptiness.

The spiritual component or catalog of meritorious character is quite enough evidence that he or she is certainly good enough and sufficient. In a way of life that values *who* a person is, moral clarity, discipline, and fortitude become the vanguards that protect an individual's credibility and relevance. The person looks forward to being vulnerable with grace and humility, which opens a pathway for authenticity, originality, and civility to take center stage. With this way of life, he or she quickly learns that in order to advance credibility and relevance, it is important to assist others with the same endeavor. It is important not to establish credibility for another, but to help point out the merits of value and significance that pertain to *who* that individual is internally.

In the other value system, those feelings of emptiness drive individuals to search for external rewards, none of which can fill the void. Moral ineptitude is an ever-present problem that faces any individual when credibility is consistently sought through external means. Contrary to a system of living that supports the sacredness of human life, its antithesis offers a counterfeit version of credibility based on recognition, validation, and prominence. A system of living that exclusively acknowledges *what* an individual is externally and materially opens the door for corruption and abuse to accompany the rush for a limited form of credibility.

Jean Shinoda Bolen, M.D., a psychiatrist, Jungian analyst, and an internationally known author and speaker, states in her book, *The Ring of Power*:

> Power is the ruling principle in patriarchy, and where power rather than love rules, freedom and justice also suffer. It is a struggle to stay with love as a principle in a patriarchal culture, yet succumbing to power is destructive to the very relationships we came into the world needing. Each individual must struggle to determine whether love or power will be the ruling principle in the psyche. Which will decide our significant

relationships choice of work, place to live and ultimately, through our choices, what we become.[17]

To add to these words, if the development of substantive character
is lacking in a patriarchal or matriarchal system of living, love will
have no chance to be considered as a ruling principle since power
will be the choice by default.

An unfortunate fact is how humanity throughout its history has
tended to pledge an undying devotion to this particular system of living. This undying devotion continues in spite of repeatedly hearing,
witnessing, and even taking part in mean-spirited ways to undercut
and undermine the credibility of fellow human beings. There is no
way to avoid the reality of impoverishment when an individual is
lacking the education to substantive character during his or her personal development. In spite of the undying loyalty, enthusiasm, and
vulnerability devoted to a system of living principally based on the
recognition of external and material value, the result remains the
same: distrust of his or her innate richness and strength.

The main take away from this system of living is its consistent
pattern of breeding superiority, greed, and corruption, which is to
compensate for the impoverishment. The sacredness of human life
is disregarded in order to satisfy a personal quest for power, dominance, and immediate gratification. The internal beast is bellowing
out distressing internal feelings of emptiness, void, and insufficiency,
which need to be continuously fed something external or material. As
William Shakespeare so eloquently states, "Happy is your grace that
can translate the stubbornness of fortune into so quiet and so sweet a
style." Grace is much easier to personally embrace when credibility
originates and exists from within an individual.

Credibility given to an individual based on external and material

---

[17] Jean Shinoda Bolen, M.D., The Ring of Power, HarperCollins Publishers, 10 East
53rd Street, New York, NY 10022 (page 11).

criteria offers nothing close to grace, because the translation of worthiness under such circumstances is closely associated with power and
a one-dimensional use of authority. Qualities such as integrity and
civility simply do not convert into any meaningful purpose within a
way of life that honors what an individual is instead of who he or she
is inherently. "The stubbornness of fortune" will always be a common
denominator when such thinking prevails. Plus, the attempt to attain
an external fortune has an internal mechanism that will persistently
sound the alarm that enough is never simply enough.

Power and the one-dimensional use of authority will consistently
be limited to the few people who can muscle and manipulate their
way to such a tenuous summit. And coexisting alongside this form
of credibility is the ever-present need to repel any outside attempt to
usurp power and authority. So, why keep reaching for what causes
great harm to a person? And more importantly, why keep seeking
what he or she already possesses internally, but in a different and
more substantive format? These two questions are rhetorical, which
allows the reader to ponder for the answers. Once credibility is recognized and accepted on the basis of *who* an individual is regarding
his or her merits of character, the pretentious fortune simply does
not matter; it is the person who matters. Self-assurance and peace
of mind are the assured by-products of grace. It is prudent to learn
that "the stubbornness of fortune" merely exists for the stubborn.
Shakespeare was correct, "Happy is your grace."

Because grace is a combination of humility and nobility, the stubborn have a difficult time accepting this attribute of good character
as credible due to its lack of forcefulness. Though the empowered may
experience an attraction to the *who* element of the impoverished, such
as modesty and goodness; caution should be exercised. Regrettably,
this level of appreciation cannot be trusted as being genuine, because the person receiving the compliment lacks recognition of his
or her personal distinctions. Impoverishment will always seek out

impoverishment to establish relationships, not the empowered. In general, people are more comfortable seeking out the familiar. It is much easier to experience commonality than the threat of encountering transparency and vulnerability with a stranger. The impoverished has yet to recognize and accept the qualities of character the empowered have come to understand are substantive. Therefore, experiences of genuine appreciation, approval, and unconditional love are received with a great deal of skepticism. Instead of gravitating toward relationships committed to the development and growth of sound character, impoverishment manipulates its audience to maintain what is customary.

Be it one or a multitude of people the impoverished seek to manipulate, three distinct and consistent conclusions are made clear as to the structure of relationships. One conclusion is that support and recognition is one-sided, and relationships in general are not a mutual affair. The second conclusion is that communication leaves a great deal to be desired. During critical moments when conflict is present and honesty is important to bring forth, the impoverished will hold back what he or she actually would like to say. In its place, the impoverished will say what he or she does not mean, doing whatever it takes to keep away from qualities such as, accountability, vulnerability, and transparency.

Honesty expressed in conjunction with the character trait of vulnerability is absolutely avoided, and intimacy is lost. And the third conclusion, relationships are forged for no other purpose than to help insulate the impoverished from clearly hearing and responding appropriately to the internal cry of "Please give me reason to know that I matter." This agenda has served much of humanity all too well throughout history. The agenda is comprised of establishing a strategy that provides a person with a reason that he or she matters solely based on what that individual is externally and possesses materially.

It should be added, any society, culture, or religion furnishing a person with insulation that establishes the reason he or she matters based on external and material credentials commits a miscarriage of morality. Configuring insulation on the basis of economics, race, ethnicity, and religion acts as a deterrent against a person taking responsibility to satisfy only what he or she can successfully accomplish. Learning his or her true value as an individual through the development of substantive character is a personal journey no society, culture, or religion can circumvent for any person. To do so would play a significant role in helping to create a condition of impoverishment for the person. It is appropriate to provide encouragement, unrestricted pathways, and unbiased teachings that will expand the personal quest to attain genuine credibility and relevance.

Robert A. Johnson, in his book *Owning Your Own Shadow*, adds an illuminating insight to this challenge by stating, "We all are born whole but somehow the culture demands that we live out only part of our nature and refuse other parts of our inheritance. We divide the self into an ego and a shadow because our culture insists that we behave in a particular manner."[18] Because culture refuses to educate to the merits of character translates into a responsibility the individual has to take on to reclaim his or her personal wholeness and legitimacy. The shadow can then claim an inheritance of genuine credibility and relevance.

Only when experiences have reached a painful conclusion coupled with the lack of success attached to personal ventures can a reversal of misfortune begin in earnest. Through a process of self-examination, a person can understand where the lack of success originated. Personal undertakings generally deserving a complete and thorough review can be failure with one or more marriages, difficulty raising children to be responsible and respectful, long-term discontent with career

---

[18] Robert A. Johnson, Owning Your Own Shadow, HarperCollins Publishers, 10 East 53rd Street, New York, NY 10022 (pg. 10).

and employment, and/or the collapse of credit and money management. A principal reason for the "stubbornness of fortune," rather than "the grace that can translate into so quiet and so sweet a style" can be easily understood.

The approach is to first examine the underlying motivation regarding personal preference and choice. More often than not, marriage, children, romance, career, job, beauty, religion, political affiliation, athletics, and finances are chosen as a source for security, stability, credibility, and relevance. Once such external factors are viewed in this manner, what arrives next is the investment of personal faith. And with faith comes a mind-set involving expectations and conditions. Rather than faith in the strength and composition of character as the source of existence, the external and material are inserted as the source for credibility.

Preference and choice are generally restricted to the familiar, such as class, race, ethnicity, and religion. The field from which to choose is limited, narrow, and short on providing sustainable credibility and relevance. And, since the individual instinctively reacts to the internal need, "Please give me reason to know that I matter," he or she chooses an external source that expects total allegiance in exchange for validation. Race, ethnic, gender, and religious inequalities offer validation for those in positions of power in exchange for the soul of the individual. Without the foundation of character development to fall back on that would define personal relevance and credibility, the urge is to satisfy the need as best as he or she can.

Impoverishment makes its presence felt with the development of a self-indulgent and self-important approach to living his or her life. Credibility and relevance are solely based on *what* an individual is externally and materially. However, the recognition, acceptance, and credibility received does little to quiet the internal need for authenticity, both from within and from relationships. The person, the soul, can simply reach a point where he or she cannot digest more external food that has nothing in common with satisfying the internal hunger. To seek credibility and relevance to satisfy the lie that he or she does not matter unless certain external and material accomplishments are achieved creates a foundation for the "stubbornness of fortune" to establish itself.

It makes sense that a person would go outside of him or herself to pursue credibility and relevance when personally deficient in the education of substantive character. The lack of awareness that a meaningless pursuit is underway to satisfy external standards that ignore the value of *who* an individual is regarding intrinsic merit is more than enough to propel the journey. The ability to stop the quest cannot occur until the day arrives when the realization becomes clear that no amount of effort can stop the disappointment and frustration of never being quite good enough to satisfy standards that ignore the value of *who* an individual is with respect to innate merit. To support a system of living that can promise moral clarity, discipline, and fortitude based on accountability, mutual consideration, and personal responsibility is an easy choice for the empowered.

Integrity offers life and stability to the individual, to the soul that exists within each individual. Educate an individual to the merits and value of his or her character and he or she will have reason to know that he or she matters. The inherent gifts of character morally and substantively not only elevate the individual, but also allow for a different narrative to be added through demonstration that balances a way of life dominated by external and material value. The merits of an individual's character are what substantiates human life and supports the sanctity of that life. One can say with certainty, educate an individual to the merits and value of his or her character and the staying power of impoverishment quietly diminishes.

Jean Shinoda Bolen, M.D., speaks rather convincingly in her book *The Ring of Power* about the issue of credibility. She states:

I am convinced that we enter the world seeking to be loved and that we settle for power when we are not loved. The world we enter is a world of relationships. At birth, we arrive in our innocence and vulnerability as babies, designed to evoke the love and nurturing that we need to survive. After birth, life unfolds in a spiral pattern: we repeatedly enter new worlds of relationships—as children, as adolescents, and as adults—each time wanting to be welcomed into this new world and loved. When we find that we are not loved or are loved only for what we do or what we own, power in some form becomes the substitute, the means by which we seek acceptance and security that love provides freely. Thus we seek to be noticed or needed, to be indispensable or in control.[19]

The best form of love any individual can experience is expressed through a process of education with regard to the inherent gifts of his or her character.

To conclude this section, a review of certain key statements made throughout this chapter will be reexamined. It is important to understand that impoverishment attempts to substantiate the lie that there is a shortage of relevance and credibility. The lie also suggests that only a few individuals and groups satisfy specific qualifications to be recognized as being credible and relevant. What an individual is externally and materially is the measuring stick that determines relevancy and credibility, not who that individual is with respect to meritorious character. If a person is unable to join the ranks of the powerful and prominent, or even align him or herself with this socially elite faction, the outcome is predictable.

---

[19] Jean Shinoda Bolen, M.D., The Ring of Power, HarperCollins Publishers, 10 East 53rd Street, New York, NY 10022 (page 10).

The internal struggle for legitimacy looms large in order to maintain a credible self-perception. Even though the pseudo-powerful and prominent are elevated through class, race, ethnicity, beauty, education, and religion, ineptitude and irrelevance remain as constant bedfellows. And, of course, if the person remains unaware of his or her inherent gifts of character, then the pursuit to become powerful and controlling moves to becomes an obsession. It is not until the insulation afforded to *what* he or she is externally and materially begins to wear thin, due to the ever-fickle standards of the external world, that a person realizes how little was received in turn for the soul.

The disenfranchised, homeless, depressed, and addicted have two game-changing decisions in common: all have chosen to remain victimized by misinformation and to internalize the blame for experiences culminating into personal irrelevancy and the loss of credibility. Rather than take responsibility for colliding with an unprincipled way of life and its value system and for not successfully fitting into a scheme they were never intended to fit inside, the course chosen leaves no room for self-redemption. These individuals have staggered into an existence largely consumed with self-condemnation and perpetual anguish.

Rather than remain in the midst of a conventional life, but from a more advantageous position of strength as calculated by a different value system, many individuals have chosen to be, and stay, marginalized. Lacking the education and knowledge that there is another value system to commit one's self to that represents a way of life that would measure relevancy and credibility more appropriately, an ugly historical point is repeated. Due to using misinformation relative to a flawed perception of human life, the loss and disappearance of relevant and precious human lives continues to depress and impede the moral advancement of humanity.

Teach a man, woman, and child how to feed his or her soul through the development and practice of sound character and the presence of impoverishment as acted through violence, hatred, resentment, and comparison fades to the background of humanity's landscape. Evil and its intent to discredit and destroy loses its grip on humanity's willingness to compromise innate strength for deception and betrayal. Teach a man, woman, and child to develop and practice his or her merits of character and the presence of harmful dependencies, whether related to government, state, friendship, or family, lessens dramatically. Impoverishment and counterproductive dependencies are replaced with an appreciation and understanding of the importance of developing interdependence. Educate an individual to character and he or she will begin to see through a different lens the actual foundation for credibility, relevancy, and personal value. Where and how the true value of a human life is achieved will be understood. Just as important, that same individual is able to take a significant step toward self-forgiveness and absolution for having engaged in a way of life that negated and undermined the sanctity of human life, and the qualities that represented substantive character.

The act of self-betrayal and betrayal of others will illustrate the state of impoverishment. And as an individual embraces its opposite, self-forgiveness and humility act as the varnish to help protect the progress in becoming the best person that he or she can achieve. Self-empowerment arising through the development of his or her merits of character is the chosen accomplishment. As the late John (Jay) McCloy, a U.S. government official, lawyer, and diplomat stated, "Humility leads to strength and not to weakness. It is the highest form of self-respect to admit mistakes and to make amends for them." Once again, educate to character and children will stop taking guns to school to prove their relevance, or to resolve conflict.

Educate to character and children will stop shooting and murdering other children. Educate to character and children will stop acting out sexually and having babies to feel loved and prove that they have credibility. When the adults who are charged with parenting and mentoring these young lives have been educated to understand and acknowledge the value and significance of human life through the gateway of meritorious character development, a miraculous moment appears. Three excellent qualities that represent sound character—integrity, civility, and personal responsibility—will increasingly act as deterrents against children being considered and treated as irrelevant.

It is quite unsettling to listen, time and time again, to the vigorous rhetoric expressed, especially by politicians during presidential elections. The argument always centers on the need to leave the next generation a sound and stable financial picture. Nothing is ever mentioned about the importance of leaving the next generation a sound and stable moral structure, one that educates and values the merits of character. It is paradoxical to ignore and negate the one true path to establishing substantive credibility, then spend each waking day seeking ways and means to destroy the credibility of oneself and others—using class, race, ethnic, religious, gender, and age as weapons to do so. Humanity has shown throughout its history a propensity to devour and destroy its own through financial greed; declared and undeclared wars; child abuse; hatred and contempt for religious, secular, ethnic, race, class, and gender differences.

The condition of impoverishment exists because the value of character does not exist beyond mere clichés and talking points to actually elevate the human experience from a sheer moral standpoint. On the political stage, the far right and far left, liberal and conservative alike, join with fundamentalist religious and racial purists to devour and destroy that which is different. Interdependence and compromise are certainly out of the question to the impoverished. The lack of use regarding merits of character such as civility and integrity are continuously on display to evidence a state of impoverishment due to an agenda that is based on pure selfish gain, and at the expense of other people.

Lastly, it is important that every effort be made to educate to the recognition and value of the inherent gifts of meritorious character in order to diminish the negative impact arising from impoverishment. When it is understood that the primary focus on achieving credibility includes the development of an individual's internal credentials, impoverishment will diminish. Sustainable and meaningful credibility has absolutely nothing to do with *what* an individual is externally, what an individual owns or anticipates coming into possession of regarding material value. In the end, a way of life and its value systems that ignore *who* an individual is in terms of character is a structure that will collapse upon itself due to the inability to put distance between what is driven by self-importance and self-indulgence and what is honorably supported by the influence of integrity.

The collapse is primarily due to the destabilization of moral clarity, discipline, and fortitude. And any relationship, family, ethnicity, culture, or nation that is principally established on such a shallow way of life is destined to eventually collapse under weak and feeble foundations. When neglecting to learn and teach the importance of sound character, the sacredness of human life and the lack of ethics will always be a problem impeding humanity's moral advancement. Psychotherapist Alice Miller, in her book *The Banished Knowledge*, states, "It is not true that evil, destructiveness, and perversion inevitably form part of the human existence, no matter how often this is maintained, but it is true that we are daily producing more evil and with it an ocean of suffering for millions that is absolutely avoidable."[20]

It is important to note, a nation such as America that preaches

---

[20] Alice Miller, *The Banished Knowledge*, Bantam Doubleday Dell Publishing Group, Inc., 666 Fifth Avenue, New York, NY 10103 (page 143).

daily about the importance of accumulating material wealth and prosperity, the notion that its populace is significantly impacted by a condition of impoverishment in many minds is an absurdity. The reality of such a condition will not be an easily accepted assertion by most readers. Expand that perspective to include the global community, and there is ample evidence to support the observation that the condition of impoverishment has humanity in a deathlike grip. But, doubt and disbelief will be the response to such an observation. Absurd or not, the truth that impoverishment is perpetuating the abuse of power throughout the global community is upon us. It is time to act boldly and with conviction to diminish its harmful effect. The refusal to address the negative effects impoverishment is having worldwide and nationally is widening the ocean of human suffering for millions of people.

It should be made clear that there can never be the expectation of eliminating impoverishment from the human landscape completely. There will always be individuals who seek to benefit from what he or she is externally and materially. In fact, it is assumed by some to be an easier path to take toward achieving credibility, irrespective of the consequences. But, one fact is known—when humanity firmly understands that personal credibility is strictly derived on the basis of *who* an individual is in terms of his or her merits of character, the tears can stop flowing. The bleeding will have decreased greatly as the numbers of innocent lives sacrificed for absolutely nothing will have lessened.

I leave you with one final thought. Alice Miller, in her book *The Untouched Key,* also says:

> People whose integrity has not been damaged in childhood, who were protected, respected, and treated with honesty by their parents, will be, both in their youth and adulthood, intelligent, responsive,

empathetic, and highly sensitive. They will take pleasure in life and will not feel any need to kill or even hurt others or themselves. They will use their power to defend themselves but not to attack others. They will not be able to do otherwise than to respect and protect those weaker than themselves, including their children, because this is what they have learned from their own experiences and because it is this knowledge and not the experience of cruelty that has been stored up inside them from the beginning.[21]

Integrity will always reflect the soundness and good derived from the development of meritorious character.

---

[21] Alice Miller, *The Untouched Key*, Bantam Doubleday Dell Publishing Group, Inc., 666 Fifth Avenue, New York, NY 10103 (page 170).

Chapter Nine

CONCLUSION

A Native American elder described his own inner struggles this way: "Inside of me there are two dogs. One of the dogs is mean and evil. The other dog is good. The mean dog fights the good dog all the time." When asked which dog wins, he reflected for a moment and replied, "The one I feed the most."

Unknown

By the time a person has finally figured out that the tooth fairy, Easter Bunny, and Santa Claus live down the hall in the master bedroom, he or she has figured out a few other long-standing folk-lores.[22] However, one significant cross-cultural myth continues to remain mystifying, and it is the one that links accommodation and performance with bona fide credibility. Relationships that base the credibility of an individual on his or her ability to accommodate and perform to external expectations run the risk of inviting deception

---

[22] http://literarydevices.net/folklore/; Folklore is a collection of fictional stories about animals and people, of cultural myths, jokes, songs, tales and even quotes. It is a description of culture, which has passed down verbally from generation to generation in any written or oral form. Although some folklores depict universal truths, it is also that unfounded beliefs and superstitions are basic elements of folklore tradition.

and cheating as a means to achieve recognition. When to be good and to do good is to satisfy the needs of external sources, rather than to express the inherent gifts of character that reveal genuine credibility, the pretense is obvious. Obedience and collaboration are not virtues representative of an internal accord, but a fear of rejection. Disobedience and contrary can be reactions to assumptions made that compliance should be automatic. Even though the expectations of compliance have nothing to do with recognizing or advancing the legitimate needs of the individual, adaptation and execution are expected.

It is true; accommodation and performance provide a basic function for any relationship. When attention to the properties of good character are lacking or deemed irrelevant, the formation of the relationship can become complicated. With this deficiency, the undertaking to accommodate and perform will mainly fall on the shoulders of the least empowered or needier to carry out. The relationship is imbalanced, because one side of the connection is willing to relinquish his or her passion, autonomy, individuality, convictions, and authority for the purpose of promoting the identical qualities on the other side of the partnership. The underlying motivation for a person or group to pursue this form of practice is to attain credibility and relevance.

Even though the credibility and relevance is conditional and minimum at best, something is better than nothing when self-perception is lacking in personal qualities of merit. The underlying incentive for a person to attract this form of practice is simple: to attain power and domination. Credibility and relevance are placed above the person or group offering to renounce self-fulfillment in exchange for external validation. Authoritarian rule, romantic relationships, the decision to have children, and the institutions of family, marriage, religion, and politics are, to a great extent, influenced by the practice of accommodation and performance.

Class, race, ethnic, and gender warfare have been fought over the ideology that accommodation and performance is a sure way to achieve credibility and relevance. Such a practice also induces the idea that it is in the best interest of the individual or group adapting and carrying out the expectations "to go along, to get along." Since character development has never been determined to be a critical issue for humanity to address, this is a major reason for the longevity this practice has experienced. Also encouraged by power notables is the overt, and oftentimes, covert, message to mute any questioning of authority if the limited form of credibility and relevance are not to be jeopardized.

Though there is no seating at the table of importance, accommodation and performance cannot be threatened. As long as the development of a person's merits of character continues to be a non-concern, relationships remain imbalanced. It is no secret, when history is examined, that iconic figures such as Jesus, Mahatma Gandhi, and the Reverend Doctor Martin Luther King Jr. disputed the practice of accommodation and performance within their respective cultures. Aside from these high-profile individuals, there are, and have been, many heroes stepping up to challenge inequities and inequalities assembled on the accommodation and performance model. It is no secret all such heroes were either imprisoned or assassinated for their efforts to introduce mutuality and equality into the human equation of engagement.

Under the conditions of mutuality, coalition, and integrity building, accommodation and performance are expected to be in play, but under very different circumstances as just described. The difference is easily detectable, because there is a genuine interest in the individual. Other than *what* a person is externally and possesses materially, *who* that person is inherently in terms of character brings balance to his or her life.

Where credibility is measured by the development and practice of the inherent gifts of character, the maturation of his or her moral aptitude can be inspiring to others. Accommodation and performance are used as a means to encourage and support other individuals to be the best that he or she can be in terms of good character.

Relationship-wise, each partner naturally creates space at the table of importance, because each understands no one individual or group has a lock on intelligence, knowledge, and wisdom. There are numerous religious principles, political viewpoints, nationalistic ideologies, regional preferences, racial and ethnic beliefs. Though the differences are plenty, the commonalities are greater in terms of inherent credibility and relevance. Because intelligence, knowledge, and wisdom are infinite, not finite, human differences enhance the opportunity to learn from one another with a tide of understanding that truly lifts all boats. The gifts of character and an individuality protected by such gifts make certain the principal and principle of good are the underpinnings of the relationship. There is no such ethic in play that encourages a person to seek or demand from another person what he or she refuses to give to another.

To teach a form of credibility that includes the type of accommodation and performance that takes precedence over the character development of a person is to pass on what is conditional and provisional, at best. No matter how innocent and well-intended the educational process, the end result is to teach the basis of pretense. To ensure that credibility and relevance are never in jeopardy of being lost, a person will often attempt to make him or herself to appear different than what is simply true. Because this model of accommodation and performance lacks guidance from the qualities of substantive character, a person can act as if it is love that he or she feels for a partner. Pretense can portray a belief in God due to church affiliation; he or she is not a racist when it is prejudice toward different races that fills the heart or contempt for the poor while donating to sympathizing charitable organizations, and looking good when the tooth fairy, Easter Bunny, and Santa Claus are about to appear.

The folklore that suggests accommodation and performance can bring about credibility remains mystifying because the learning process supports the notion that pretense is far better than the genuine and authentic. Mystifying, because the meager gains from this model in exchange for individuality, passion, authority, and equality are never questioned as to why a deficit return. Mystifying, because of the countless experiences resulting in disappointment for giving years of loyalty to a system of living promising lasting credibility only provided more inequality and inequity. The marriage, children, extended family, dream home, prestigious career, religion, and political affiliation all faded into a deep shadow of mediocrity. The question that does seem to surface is one of reflection, "Where was I, the person, in all this accommodating and performing?"

Without question, learning to portray what appears to be good, rather than learning to embody the merits of character can attain some measure of conditional credibility and relevance. Thus, accommodation and performance will be deemed acceptable in terms of providing a pretense of good. When a person attains some measure of credibility and relevance with the purpose of satisfying an external standard, the lack of fulfillment can be an end result. He or she will have a difficult time feeling internally satisfied, because the quest had nothing to do with him or her personally. Pretense can be but to simply live within him or herself with respect to *who* he or she is inherently. Being committed to achieving credibility and relevance based on how well he or she satisfies the needs of others is similar to chasing the carrot at the end of the legendary stick. It is a process that is never-ending for those that consider themselves to be breathless.

From the moment a person awakes in the morning to the moment of falling asleep at bedtime, he or she will have spent a great deal of time wrestling and struggling with one nagging thought. As most would agree, the issues of credibility and relevance are a natural human instinct. Hopefully, as he or she prepares to fall asleep from that day's activities, he or she is satisfied with its achievement. It is not uncommon for the preceding daytime activities to intensify during the midnight hour of sleep when he or she is less than satisfied with the results. "Did I meet my sales or production quota for the day to validate my credibility?" "Was I successful with satisfying the wants and needs of my parishioners, community, or constituents to justify being in a religious, civic, or political position of leadership?"

"Did I purchase the right suit, dress, automobile, condominium, or home to boost my credibility?" "Am I attractive enough, loved enough, and have I had enough sex to substantiate that I am relevant and credible?" "Are the children showing enough respect toward me as their parent to merit credibility beyond the fact that I am capable of having or adopting a child?" "Have I scored enough baskets, gotten enough hits, scored enough touchdowns to prove my credibility and relevance with respect to being on the team?" "What is the next vacation to be taken that will enhance my credibility among my partner and/or coworkers?"

The above are just a small sampling of the internal messages an individual will go back and forth with when attempting to determine whether he or she has measured up to achieving personal credibility or not. And this is especially true for the person fully invested in the social, cultural, economic, and religious systems that determine credibility and relevance based on *what* a person is externally and possesses materially. However, there are more convenient and conventional ways to measure if he or she is credible. Employing standards established within a system of living that are focused solely on external value will help to make such a determination. This personal gauge is best used when comparison is made to another person or group identified and singled out as being less than credible based on external standards. The person or group making the judgement naturally feels superior, relevant, valued, and more credible. Historically speaking, lines of division that help make comparisons easy to come by have existed with class, race, ethnicity, age, gender, and religious differences.

Educate to the merits of an individual's character and division becomes an obsolete reference replaced by distinction and variation. However, where superior and inferior claims are made due to inequality and inequity, a commonly known axiom comes into play: "the sword can cut on both sides." For different reasons, but serving the same purpose, many individuals who have fallen through the cracks of society will often view their credibility and relevance as little to nothing. Without the additional personal information provided through character development, difficult economic, physical, psychological, and spiritual experiences become the only way a person will define him or herself. Lacking the education can make it quite challenging to accept the idea that he or she is in possession of the innate gifts of resourcefulness and self-reliance. To be receptive to the concepts of an inherent credibility and relevance that expand self-perception can be too high of a reach without at least an openness to character development.

Conspiring with a system of living by accepting one of its propositions that experiences, good or bad, define a person is extremely reckless. This is a self-defeating principle to embrace, because the system offers no alternative to defining oneself other than through experiences burdened with inequities and inequalities. Educate an individual to an expanded self-perception through the development of the honorable traits of character and multiforms for defining oneself open up. To collude with a system that solely promotes credibility based external and material value is absolutely absurd. At the time seductive advertisements flood media outlets, this system knows exactly how unsuccessful individuals in their failed attempts to achieve this form of credibility will personally interpret such efforts. Again, there is no concern for the sanctity of an individual when the development of meritorious character is not included in the respective system of living.

Inequities and inequalities charm both the advantaged and disadvantaged by establishing the idea that credibility is restricted to a few and lies with the dominant and powerful. Even though many individuals know this, yet the attempt is made to enter the circle and enjoy sitting at the table of importance reserved for only a few. The disadvantaged practice the same methods of attaining credibility though dominance and power, as do the advantaged. With the education to substantive character absent from the landscape, the seduction of power is elevated to a more persuasive level. To live below the poverty line in any society, to accept chronic unemployment, alcoholism, drug addiction, homelessness, depression, eating disorders, and living without health insurance is difficult to stop without knowing the valid reasons to do so.

Due to this difficulty with accepting an inherent credibility that is outside external and material value, the individual or group will pursue the only available alternate. The quest involves looking for confirmation of his or her inferior status by seeking relief from the system and people that helped to engineer self-betrayal. This is mainly an unconscious decision. A first instinct is to seek validation for a self-perception of inferiority from people who benefit and support the external value system. Style of dress, antisocial behavior, and blame for a lifestyle that supports an inferior status are common ways to seek relief and validation. This is especially true when a person or group has virtually no knowledge concerning his or her internal assets. As a result of this lack of information, the person or group remains physically, emotionally, psychologically, and spiritually invested in a value system that is imbalanced and corrupt.

For the advantaged, rather than help establish an educational process that teaches a man, woman, or child to be self-reliant through character development, the opposite occurs. Dependency and contempt are the remedies received from an external and material-based system of living. Power and domination are not interested in sharing credibility and relevance. There is no interest in sharing importance and authority derived from economic, race, ethnic, educational, gender, and religious inequities and inequalities. If character development was part of the overall landscape, there would be no interest in wanting to share the spoils derived from imbalance and corruption. Receiving monthly food stamps, Medicare and Medicaid, welfare checks, or other forms of government-funded economic assistance can provide a measure of limited credibility. But, when stacked up against a self-perception overshadowed by a sense of inferiority, little comfort can be found. This can be of little consequence to reverse a collaborative effort designed to sustain a personal sense of inadequacy and dependence versus that of self-determination.

While the advantaged use a side of the proverbial sword to elevate and feel superior with respect to credibility being based on external and material value, the disadvantaged use the other side to deflate and feel inferior. What both have in common is that neither group will take up the sword to create and carve out a different way of life that is mutually beneficial to the groups as a whole. Neither will take responsibility to create a system of living that includes an education that honors the best humanity has to offer itself on an individual basis. And just as important, a system of living that includes offering the best to one another regarding the inherent gifts of an individual's character. Roadside casualties and fatalities belonging to real human beings remain as a moral blight on humanity's historical reputation of self-inflicted injury and harm.

What is revealed is a history of humankind joining forces with one another to create and uphold social, cultural, economic, and religious systems of living that fail to teach the sanctity of human life. This is in principle conducted by ignoring and preventing the teaching of an individual's inherent gifts of character. Integrity, ingenuity, dignity, and community, which are necessary to build a strong moral infrastructure, are absent from the ethical diet on both sides of the advantaged and disadvantaged equation. A significant life lesson is disregarded when character development is not a focal point of the education format. And that life lesson happens to be how the daily goal of each individual is not only to protect and preserve the dignity of one's self, but to extend that same daily commitment and credibility to his or her fellow human.

An individual must be taught at an early age to welcome this life lesson by learning of his or her merits of character; otherwise, it can generally take a lifetime to learn of its importance and magnitude. Usually, this never-to-be-forgettable lesson rises to a level of consciousness through relationships that are, at its core, painful and ineffective. To principally measure credibility based on external and material value is to invest in a way of life established on self-importance and self-indulgence. Leaving out the development of one's merits of character ensures that power and control are the means of engagement. Such a foundation is doomed to adversely plague the best efforts of any well-intended, but ill-advised way of life. It is no secret power corrupts and absolute power will absolutely corrupt. This unprincipled way of life is further intensified by efforts to preserve measures that make certain those on the periphery and in pursuit of this form of sustainable credibility fall through built-in cracks designed by inequity and inequality. It is time that humankind stop seeking the type of credibility and relevance that robs the soul of an opportunity to truly advance the sacredness of human life.

Standards based on deceit, deception, and fraud designed to advance economic, racial, ethnic, religious, and gender disparities are kept in place to make certain various segments of humanity can never quite measure up to a manufactured level of credibility. The truth is, there is only so much recognition and affirmation to go around when personal value is solely based on an individual's external and material value. It is also time for segments of humanity not measuring up to duplicitous standards to seek a more viable means to experience importance and relevance. Getting caught up in the so-called only show in town in defining oneself through experiences is eliminated because a more practical means to accomplish this feat is currently available. The development of character allows an individual to gladly accept this fact and acknowledge that there are enough leaders to go around. In conjunction with this, the development of character also allows a person to know there is always room for the demonstration and example of leadership.

An unspoken value that is attributed to demonstrating his or her merits of character is how this practice consistently acts as a safeguard and a reminder of one sensible and important fact. A person need not strive to be more than *what* he or she is externally and possesses materially, and certainly not accept being less than *who* he or she is in terms of sound character. When the centerpiece of his or her personal canvas reflects the imitation of another individual or a popular myth, another important fact is revealed. Overshadowing his or her individuality expressive of good character with deception and manipulation distorts the entire personal canvas. Seeking to please and accommodate customs, traditions, rituals, and significant others in order to achieve a conditional and unsustainable credibility runs a limited course in terms of personal satisfaction.

Lacking information as to where and how genuine credibility is initiated opens the door for an old axiom to gain importance. The proclamation reads, "the more things change, the more they remain the same." Instead of a new Band-Aid or the rearranging of the deck chairs to bring about the change that removes "the more they remain the same" requires an inclusion of the qualities of good character into the problem-solving process. Such an approach eliminates the influence of special interest to maintain the problem, but gives the appearance a solution is being sought. Whether the problem is economic, social, political, racial, ethnic, religious, or personal, the attributes of sound character will produce results that are beneficial to all parties involved.

The worn-out attempt to legislate behavior that mandates one group of people to act respectful toward another group of people will never legislate morality.

The high incarceration rate of black and brown people, abortion, alcohol and drug addiction, homelessness, terrorism, hate crimes, poverty . . . These and other social adversities begin to decline when individuals caught in the web of depravity are willing to use a more effective approach to resolve respective distresses. When the inclusion of teachings regarding inherent and genuine credibility is inserted into the educational format, the need to compulsively legislate morality also decreases. Attempts to prolong the life of inequities and inequalities are not considered a course of action. A person will have discovered more options to define him or herself as a result of character development. The ability to expand on self-perception through the qualities of good character, rather than to be limited by experiences, removes the harmful edge to inequities and inequalities.

A moral infrastructure deficient in a conviction to live by the properties of integrity, which include accountability, mutual consideration, and personal responsibility, heightens the likelihood of an unpleasant experience. The deficiency makes it virtually impossible for a person to adequately protect him or herself. This happens to be the norm when committed to a system of living that primarily establishes credibility on external and material credentials. Because this same system of living breeds deception, deceit, and manipulation in order to decorate the *what* factors, it becomes extremely difficult to know when truth and trust are being expressed. A person seeking to establish credibility and relevance by living his or her life principally by the qualities of good character representative of *who* he or she is inherently achieves a huge feat. He or she elevates the *what* status without relying upon or becoming dependent on external and material criterion, such as race, ethnicity, gender, economics, or religion.

It is wise to prepare for a lukewarm response and support from individuals who fundamentally rely upon and are dependent on external and material criterion for credibility. Because the focus to attain credibility and relevance is outwardly driven, the pursuit consistently finds a person affirming and confirming the negative. The individual is locked into an endless mind-set of lack, because wholeness and completeness is based on external and material criterion. Power and control are always in need of more power and control, whereas, through character development, a person comes to understand that wholeness and completeness are based on his or her inherent credibility.

To live life based on his or her merits of character are what actually establish credibility and relevance on this plane of existence. The pathway to the opposite of relevance is always lurking in the background. Indicators, such as greed, corruption, abuse, and deceit, reveal that a moral crisis is underway. When personal meaning and purpose are exclusively outward and materially based, the temptation to be more than *what* an individual is guarantees an eventual fall from grace: albeit, a major or lesser error in judgment. The personal cost for being less than *who* an individual is regarding living the qualities that represent good character has consistently been humiliation, disgrace, and the loss of credibility.

In conclusion, to transition out of a system of living that promotes the belief there is sustainable credibility and relevance through the attainment of power and authority will require a vast effort. A willingness coupled with a sense of urgency to repair a broken value system becomes the first order of business. Expanding an external and material value system to include the inherent value of the qualities comprising good character accomplishes one significant goal. Humanity moves to an unprecedented level of moral aptitude by ensuring that credibility and relevance represent balanced depictions for an individual to attain. The urgency results from an understanding there is no benefit for any person to voluntarily accept a position on an imbalanced playing field with respect to relationships. Irrespective of where an individual resides, not a day goes by he or she is not flooded with external messages that to avoid inadequacy, credibility is attained primarily through external and material means. The organs most used to accomplish this message are the usual suspects: class, race, ethnicity, religion, consumerism, and aesthetic value for the physical.

Consistent with a system of living solely based on external and material value are the deliberate attempts to create reasons for an individual to develop a false appetite. On a twenty-four-hour/seven-day cycle, rationale is presented to the consumer with the encouragement to invest in elevating his or her external and material standing. Invest in looking beautiful or handsome, owning a new automobile or credit card, the ability to prolong sexual pleasure, drink the best beer ever, or risk feeling irrelevant and insufficient . . .With a lack of information on the other side that speaks to the substance of sound character creating credibility, self-perception is influenced by external and material standards. The floodgates open to the unjust practices derived from inequities and inequalities, as humankind rushes to feel adequate and sufficient. Character development teaches an individual the qualities of being adequate and sufficient are inherent gifts that go beyond the range or limits of feelings.

To transition from historically based imbalanced playing fields, such as class, race, ethnicity, gender, religion, jobs, and education, to a playing field that is balanced, an important step is taken. A person has to come to terms with genuine credibility beginning with the recognition that his or her merits of character are of value and relevant. This is also where and when the balanced playing field appears, one that is just and mutual. To successfully transition from self-imposed limitations that attempt to determine an individual's worth based on external and material value, substantive character is the key that opens the doors of confinement. A way of life that solely recognizes a person's worth based on external and material value will also make the attempt to marginalize and even go so far as to discourage an educational format of character development.

When it is understood that personal credibility has categorically nothing to do with any external or material standard, the sacredness of human life will elevate to a level of bona fide credibility. At the same time, what will also be understood is that personal credibility has categorically everything to do with developing the inherent gifts of an individual's character. For humanity to take the necessary steps to decisively educate to character moves this perception from theory to actuality. It is universally accepted that water and food are vital to an individual's physical well-being.

On another level, each and every individual will seek the experience of credibility because it is vital to his or her emotional and psychological well-being. And yet, humanity has demonstrated a preference for ignoring the development of character where genuine credibility is derived in favor of destroying and marginalizing the credibility of its neighbor. The failure of humankind to understand that to destroy the credibility of another is to destroy one's own credibility is the reason civilizations rise and eventually fall. It is important to make the connection that if substantive character is not developed, then it is impossible to establish moral clarity, moral discipline, and moral fortitude.

Luke Turpeinen, quoted at the beginning of Chapter Five, stated the following to this author:

> There is a problem in our society, one that affects everyone at every level and strata of our culture. The problem is a systemic lack of respect. The rich have no respect for the determination and struggles of the working class. The poor have no respect for the middle class and the luxuries they have obtained. The suburban middle class respects none but themselves

as they seek to compete with each other over petty status symbols that ultimately mean nothing. This problem exists on the streets, in our schools, and at our workplaces. Corporate management does not relate to the day-to-day problems of those that 'work the floor,' and workers don't know the complexities of decisions made by the management: only the results. This lack of respect, consideration, and willingness to appreciate the difficulties of others creates a tremendous amount of strife. Without establishing bonds of mutual respect across the different social strata, our American culture will continue to exist in strife and struggle against itself.

The following is a response to Mr. Turpeinen's comments. It is unreasonable to expect that a nation, community, or even a family can rise to the level of mutual respect while living within a system or way of life that predominantly values *what* an individual is externally and materially. Everyone within that system or way of life is fighting for the same territory, which recognizes credibility and relevance to be determined by external and material worth. The race to the top has room for just a few, while the race to the bottom has plenty of room for those who simply do not qualify. "Establishing bonds of mutual respect across the different social strata" is a virtual impossibility, because the playing field on which individuals engage one another is imbalanced. Everyone is attempting to gain an advantage over the other. This is why class, race, ethnicity, politics, religion, age, and gender are traditionally used as weapons to divide and conquer for the marathon run to the top.

As an appreciation for the education and development of the merits of an individual's inherent gifts of character expands, territory beyond the borders of external and material value takes on a more substantive meaning. As empires reach a certain point in their evo-lution, the value given to honorable character diminishes. Whereas, within a coalition of equals, meritorious character is the strapping that connects and sustains relationships within any province of peo-ple, replacing fear, dread, deceit, and treachery. Empires eventually fall, as history has recorded, because the mean and evil dog has succeeded in overtaking the good dog. The adverse response to the principles of character and its subsequent disappearance severely will minimize the emergence of moral clarity, discipline, and fortitude. A coalition of equals will maintain its longevity and credibility be-cause the good dog, the merits of character, is valued far more than self-importance and self-indulgence. Every individual has credibility by the very nature of his or her being. When humanity takes up the initiative to educate to character, more and more individuals will learn this solemn truth, as well as learn that the playing field can be indeed balanced.

The effort is not to change the world, for there is only one source that can accomplish this feat. Instead, the effort is to contribute to this plane of existence the many lessons learned from experiences that attempt to define and plot a course thought to be destiny. However, the destiny of an individual cannot be seriously considered without taking into account the one element that actually provides an oppor-tunity to be successful at being *who* he or she is on an intrinsic level. The development and practice of an individual's merits of character provides this success. To be good and to do good is disrupted when self-interest enters into the equation of living his or her life. Character ensures that the concern for interest certainly includes the individual, as well as individuals who are also part of the human network.

*If you want to run fast, run alone; if you
want to run far, run together.*

An African proverb

Afterword

Feelings and/or emotions can be extremely powerful, overwhelming, and influential. This is especially true when attached to unresolved and painful experiences. Nevertheless, when a person is confronted with these feelings or overwhelmed by powerful emotions, the challenge is of immense importance with respect to preserving his or her personal credibility and relevance.

Even when an experience internally appears to be reality, the truth is an individual will always personally bring far more than just feelings and emotions to any given moment.

One solution to overcoming an internal sense of lack, nagging depression, anxiety, or panic is to retreat to one's "secret garden" where introspective thought bears much fruit. There, he or she can be assured of comfort arriving in the form of compassion, empathy, forgiveness, and love. An individual's personal authority, authorship, and credibility are firmly established when a more reliable source is used to define oneself, other than through experiences.

The development and practice of the merits of character is that source able to teach a person he or she will always be greater than the feelings and/or emotions at any given moment. Being rooted in his or her genuine sense of good, relevance, eminence will stabilize this reality.

Lorenzo D. Leonard

Works Cited

1. Ticking Time Bomb or Demographic Dividend? Youth and Reconciliation in South Africa; South African Reconciliation Barometer Survey: 2012 Report; Kate Lefko-Everett; copyright 2012, Institute for Justice and Reconciliation; produced by COMPRESS.dsl.

2. To define one's self strictly by personal experiences that are either good, bad, or indifferent are explained in more detail in Chapter 3.

3. The statement "something is better than nothing" is explored in more detail in Chapter 3.

4. *Empires vs. Coalitions: A Defining Moment for Relationships*; Lorenzo D. Leonard; published by Strategic Book Publishing and Rights Co., 2450 Louisiana St, Houston, TX 77006, 2013; page 155, Copyright 2013.

5. *Holy Bible (Authorized King James Version) Luke*: Chapter 17:20–21,"And when he [Jesus] was demanded of the Pharisees, when the kingdom of God should come, he answered them and said, the kingdom of God cometh not with observation: Neither shall they say, lo here! or, lo there! for, behold, the kingdom of God is within you."

6. *The True Holy War, The Clash Between What We Are Externally vs. Who We Are Intrinsically*; essay on What You Are vs. Who You Are, pages 70–73; Lorenzo D. Leonard; published by Strategic Book Publishing and Rights Co., 2450 Louisiana St, Houston, TX 77006, Copyright 2009.

7. *The True Holy War, The Clash Between What We Are Externally vs. Who We Are Intrinsically*; essay on the Four Levels of Intimacy, pages 54–57; Lorenzo D. Leonard; published by Strategic Book Publishing and Rights Co., 2450 Louisiana St, Houston, TX 77006, Copyright 2009.

8. *Senate Financial Crisis Report*, 2011 (PDF). Retrieved April 22, 2011.

9. Final Report of the National Commissions on the Causes of the Financial and Economic Crisis in the United States: Official Government Edition: *The Financial Crisis Inquiry Commission*: Submitted by Pursuant to Public Law 111–21, January 2011.

10. Timothy Canova (25 November 2008), "Obamanomics: Is this real change?" The Real News. Retrieved December 13, 2008.

11. https://en.wikipedia.org/wiki/1860_United_States_Census, The United States Census of 1860 was the eighth Census conducted in the United States starting June 1, 1860 and lasting five months.

12. *Holy Bible (Authorized King James Version) Luke*: Chapter 17:20–21.

13. "Dog–eat–dog Merriam-Webster," 2008. 4 Mar. 2016 http://www.merriamwebster.com/dictionary/dog%E2%80%93eat%E2%80%93dog

14. Isacosta' Site, List of Generations Chart http://www.esds1.pt/site/images/stories/isacosta/secondary_pages/10%C2%BA_block1/ Generations%20Chart.pdf.

15. Robert A. Johnson, *Inner Work*, HarperCollins Publishers, 195 Broadway, New York, NY 10007 (page 11).

16. Robert A. Johnson, *Inner Work*, HarperCollins Publishers, 195 Broadway, New York, NY 10007 (page 10).

17. Jean Shinoda Bolen, M.D., *The Ring of Power*, HarperCollins Publishers, 195 Broadway, New York, NY 10007 (page 11).

18. Robert A. Johnson, *Owning Your Own Shadow*, HarperCollins Publishers, 195 Broadway, New York, NY 10007 (page 10).

19. Jean Shinoda Bolen, M.D., *The Ring of Power*, HarperCollins Publishers, 195 Broadway, New York, NY 10007 (page 10).

20. Alice Miller, *The Banished Knowledge*, Bantam Doubleday Dell Publishing Group, Inc., 1745 Broadway, New York, NY 10019 (page 143).

21. Alice Miller, *The Untouched Key*, Bantam Doubleday Dell Publishing Group, Inc., 1745 Broadway, New York, NY 10019 (page 170).

22. http://literarydevices.net/folklore/